Marcus Binney    Francis Machin    Ken Powell

# Bright Future
## The Re-use of Industrial Buildings

Designed by Jane Harper and John Mitchell
Picture research by Deirdre Chappell

The publication of this report has been generously sponsored by

**The Department of the Environment**
**English Heritage**
**The Baring Foundation**

Marcus Binney is president of SAVE Britain's Heritage, which he and others founded in 1975. Together with Ken Powell he organised the SAVE exhibition *Satanic Mills* in 1979. He has written for many years for *Country Life* and now writes regularly for the national press.

Ken Powell is architectural correspondent for *The Daily Telegraph*. He has served both as Northern Secretary of SAVE and subsequently as Secretary, taking a special interest in the industrial heritage.

Francis Machin RIBA is a partner in Machin Architects. The practice embraces commercial, retail, residential and urban design work, including the remodelling of historic buildings. He is also the originator of Machin Conservatories and designer of the new Mercury telephone kiosk.

The authors would like to express special thanks to Jim Buckley for his research at the start of the project, Sophie Andreae for setting the report in motion, Mark Watson for his help in Scotland, Deirdre Chappell for extensive picture research, Mark Fiennes, Peter Eley and many local authority Planning Officers for their advice and help.

*Bright Future: The Re-Use of Industrial Buildings* is published by SAVE Britain's Heritage, a registered charity (No 269129) founded in 1975 to campaign for historic buildings at risk. Copies of this and other SAVE publications are available from:

SAVE Britain's Heritage
68 Battersea High Street
London SW11 3HX
Telephone: 071-228 3336

Published April 1990

The building of
St Katharine's Dock
(c1826).

Even after years of neglect industrial buildings can retain a compelling power

## Contents

Cressbrook Mill,
Derbyshire.

# Introduction

Cressbrook Mill,
Derbyshire.

Camperdown Mill, now demolished. The chimney survives as a major Dundee landmark.

# Mills and chimneys stand magnificently in the landscape

### The Challenge

Enthusiasm for industrial architecture is a new phenomenon. Until very recently people have tended to judge industrial buildings by what they represent, rather than what they are. They have seemed the unacceptable relics of oppressive working conditions and poor living standards. The SAVE exhibition *Satanic Mills* showed clearly that industrial buildings in industrial towns were a matter of great interest and often passionate concern, not only to industrial archaeologists and conservationists, but to a very large number of people who lived in these towns and indeed had often worked in the mills.

Manningham Mills, Bradford. Disused for more than a decade it remains one of the most prominent buildings in the city. Plans have been drawn up by the owners, Lister & Co, for converting the mill into shops, offices and a hotel. Part of the complex may become a northern outstation of the Victoria & Albert Museum.

Some industrial buildings, like Marshall's Mill in Leeds or Manningham Mills in Bradford, have such monumentality, sophistication and finesse that they can be compared to the best public buildings. The majority tend to be more utilitarian but are valuable in several important ways.

First, they may be important local landmarks, simply by virtue of their size. Many have distinctive architectural features, from the Venetian windows set into the gables of early mills, to great ornamental towers and chimneys. Second, they are often very well built, particularly those which are constructed of stone. Third, they are usually very well proportioned with a satisfying rhythm of windows echoed over five storeys or more.

# Often in incomparable settings . . .

Hunslet Mill, Leeds.
A steam-powered flax
spinning mill built in 1840.
The one proud building
amidst acres of dereliction.

Their sheer size is a challenge in itself. The great Pennine textile mills were built at a time when Lancashire and Yorkshire were responsible for some 80 per cent of the world's output of cotton and wool. Even when the buildings remain in use the upper storeys tend to be empty and neglected. Most modern industry and warehousing is centred in single storey buildings. Multi-storey buildings will only survive in full commercial or industrial use in areas where space is at a premium.

Industrial use is often rough use and as the fortunes of industries and companies have declined standards of maintenance have lapsed. The surroundings of these buildings tend to be unkempt even when they are still in use. And once they are disused the whole site is taken over by the fly tipper.

Detail from the engraving
*Two Upper Cotton Works*,
published by B & J White,
1796.

Many mills and warehouses stand on the water's edge

## The Possibilities

Many industrial buildings were built to last. Their load bearing walls are solid and made to carry massive floor loadings. Like other neglected buildings they can be prey to wet and dry rot if damp gets in, but if well maintained many have a life of decades, even centuries, ahead of them.

Secondly, they are extremely adaptable. The majority are laid out on an open plan and can be repaired and upgraded for a range of uses, for light industrial and workshop use, for high-tech offices and residential accommodation.

Restored industrial buildings and industrial areas that have been transformed can develop an enormous cachet. Flats in warehouses now sell at a premium, not only in London's docklands, but in Liverpool's Albert Dock. Equally, there are many exciting examples of mills and warehouses being adapted as nursery spaces for a whole range of small businesses and individuals setting up on their own. A classic example is Dean Clough Mills in Halifax. When Ernest Hall took over this huge complex he was faced with five million square feet of empty neglected space. Within seven years he has attracted more than 200 companies, employing 2,500 people. Major companies are moving in – the Halifax Building Society, big insurance brokers and the local VAT office – precisely the kind of organisations that would normally insist on ultra modern space in a prestige new building.

Finally the setting of industrial buildings often has quite unexpected potential. Many, for example, are by water. Others have substantial areas of derelict but open land around them, offering an area of land which would rarely be available around a similar building in good condition. If this land can be attractively landscaped it becomes a major asset to a new project. Equally, it can offer exciting sites for new buildings in keeping with the original.

The message this book brings to developers, architects, surveyors and local authorities is *think big*. Those who have had the imagination and conviction to see the potential of decaying industrial buildings have been handsomely rewarded by profit as well as by accolade.

In areas of major dereliction industrial buildings and their surroundings offer a key opportunity for urban regeneration on a very large scale.

Dean Clough, Halifax, has bounced back as a small business centre.

Albert Dock, Liverpool, has been restored for shops and offices.

Tobacco Dock, London. Ingeniously adapted as a major new shopping centre for the Isle of Dogs.

Page 12: The Calder and Hebble Navigation Warehouse at Wakefield. Potentially one of the most attractive outlooks in the town.

# Decline
# and Revival

1

The Doubling Room at Dean
Mills from *The Illustrated
London News*, 1851.

The history of British industry extends back many centuries. Until the end of the 18th century, the wealth of Britain and the employment of her people were generated predominantly by agriculture, but mines and mills existed in Roman times. A nation of farmers needed iron tools. Iron was mined, and to smelt it fuel was necessary. First there was charcoal, a by-product of the forests that once covered much of the country. Then there was coal. Other metals were mined in smaller quantities – copper, lead, tin and gold (which the Romans found in Wales). The products of the agrarian society had to be processed to be of use. Grain had to be ground into flour and this could be done much more efficiently by a water-mill (which required a considerable measure of investment). So milling became a specialist trade. Wool (the chief export of medieval England) had to be spun and then woven to make cloth. This process was for centuries carried out in the homes of the farmers, but growing demand created a distinct class of weavers. As early as the 1540s, part of the old monastic church of Malmesbury Abbey was

Malmesbury Abbey, Wiltshire. Following the dissolution of the monasteries part was turned into Britain's first cloth factory.

turned into a cloth factory, with a number of people working for one entrepreneur. It was, in other words, a factory.

Early industries serviced an agrarian society. But by 1800, Britain was fast becoming an industrial society. The mines, mills and factories were overtaking the farms as a source of employment and wealth. Britain was soon to become the 'Workshop of the World'. Technological advances came thick and fast, always increasing the scale of production. The triumph of steam power broke the historic dependence on water. A ready supply of coal was the key henceforth to industrial growth. Those parts of Britain close to the coalfields became the industrial heartlands – the Midlands, Lancashire, the West Riding of Yorkshire, the North-East, southern Scotland. The old established industrial areas declined, so that today nobody thinks of Gloucestershire, East

Anglia or North Yorkshire as industrial regions. It was the age of the factory that produced the large industrial buildings which recast the face of Britain, making Oldham and Bradford, Glasgow and Sheffield, Manchester and Dundee boom towns of an unprecedented order. By 1850 all these places were, despite the social problems which arose from rapid growth, the objects of national pride. A century later, perceptions had changed. The negative effects of industry were emphasised. The Garden City ideal had become a potent legacy of British town planning, inspired, in its origins, by the thoughts of Ruskin and Morris. The evils of the industrial towns – their visual, moral and aesthetic squalor – were underlined. Modernism in architecture was an heroic creed, its agenda the restructuring of every aspect of life. Corbusier's 'Ville Radieuse' stood in startling contrast to the major cities of this country. Coketown stood condemned.

This book is about the great buildings which the so-called Industrial Revolution produced as part of its transformation of this country. They are buildings which have, until recently at least,

At Saltaire, Titus Salt laid out a model community around the mill.

Below: The mill at Saltaire has particularly striking Italianate detail.

suffered from the generally tarnished image of traditional British industry. Only now, in the midst of a new industrial revolution, are they beginning to be seriously evaluated in the way that medieval churches or Georgian country houses have been for generations. Yet, as SAVE emphasised in the introduction to *Satanic Mills* (1979), a pioneering report on Northern textile mills, factory chimneys 'are the church spires of the industrial towns'. If ingrained prejudices can be cast aside, the majesty of the buildings emerges – Battersea Power Station, Saltaire Mill, Albert Dock in Liverpool and Sleaford Maltings are nothing less than great national monuments. The industrial townscape, whether found in a modest town like Leek (Staffordshire) or Stroud (Gloucestershire) or, on a much grander scale, in Bradford or Bolton, has a validity of its own and need not be judged by the standard of a market town or garden city.

### The Problem of the Industrial Heritage

The transformation of Britain into the first fully-fledged industrial nation took place within the average human life-span. Bradford, for example, was a dozy market town of 6,000 people in 1800. Half a century later, its population had topped 100,000 and was to nearly treble again in the next 50 years. Oldham had fewer than 10,000 inhabitants in 1794, when the first textile mills began to operate there, but by the 1880s the population had reached 130,000. By 1918, there were 320 mills in Oldham. The town had nearly a third of the cotton spinning capacity of all Lancashire – its industry rivalled in size that of the entire United States.

The cotton industry thrived on a series of booms – in the 1860s, the mid '70s, the mid 1900s and (to a surprising degree) the years immediately after the First World War. But the buildings which the industry created had nothing makeshift or impermanent about them and indeed the later cotton mills of Lancashire, steel-framed and clothed in impervious red brick and terracotta, are amongst the finest industrial structures ever created in Britain. It is hardly surprising that British mill technology extended all around the world. The Oldham practice of Potts & Woodhouse, for example, designed mills in Poland and Canada. The great textile mills of north-east France are basically Lancashire mills.

If booms produced mills, slumps destroyed them. More than 180 of Oldham's mills were demolished between 1926 and 1976. The woollen and worsted industry of the West Riding of Yorkshire was less subject to this progression of boom and slump, but it has been radically

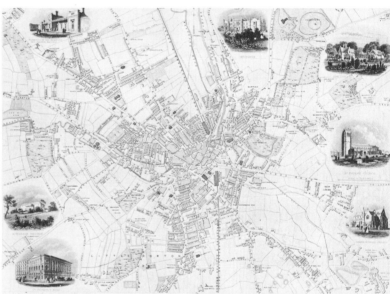

restructured since the Second World War. In 1957, 182,000 people worked in the industry. By 1976, the figure was 72,000 and there has been a further dramatic reduction in the last decade. Between 1950 and 1967, it has been estimated, over 300 mills in the West Riding became redundant and the majority were demolished. The face of industrial England has already changed dramatically.

Other industries show the same process of change at work. The woollen industry is still very much alive, with many firms making impressive profits again, but Scotland's jute industry has dwindled to very little. A century ago, it employed 40,000 people in Dundee alone (a half of the town's workforce). Its products were exported all over the world. As recently as 1950, 23 per cent of local employment was in jute. The figure is now less than three per cent . . . The decline left the Blackness area of Dundee full of empty mills. It became, according to the local authority, an

Map of Bradford c1802
Map of Bradford c1854

Page 18: Huddersfield, Yorkshire. The chimneys gave the skyline a drama the spires would never match.

Dundee's decaying jute mills should be the focus of a major programme of adaptive re-use.

No 7 Shobnall Maltings, Burton-on-Trent (demolished).

'industrial backwater'. A massive regeneration programme has now been launched to bring employment and new life to the area.

Burton-on-Trent became the brewing capital of England during the 19th century. By 1870, the breweries there covered 174 acres and there were no fewer than 104 maltings providing one of the industry's most basic raw materials. In the 1960s, major changes overtook the industry. Many smaller firms were absorbed by the 'Big Six' brewers and new production techniques made many of the old buildings redundant. Shobnall Maltings, the largest group of maltings in the world, has been largely cleared away, along with a large part of Burton's brewing heritage. The needs of the Burton breweries were served by a wide network of maltings. Bass ran the huge maltings at Sleaford, Lincolnshire, built in 1899-1905, 500,000 sq ft in area and with a frontage 1,000 feet long, which closed in 1960. The problem of a secure use for these splendid structures has yet to be resolved.

Not every 'traditional' British industry has created a legacy of fine and re-usable buildings. Coal mining, iron and steel making, and ship building occupy a prominent place in the industrial history of this country and this merits recognition. Several mining museums have, for

example, opened in former pits. But many of the steel industry buildings which have disappeared so dramatically from the face of Sheffield over the last ten years were little more than large sheds and Sheffield's own industrial museum at Kelham Island is seeking to preserve large pieces of machinery and other artefacts. There is a case for very selective preservation, in other words, but not necessarily one for creative re-use. The buildings simply do not (in most cases) adapt to the required new uses, though the extraordinary conversion of a former foundry in Birmingham, Alabama, to a theatre and shopping centre should not be ignored.

The general picture is, however, of fine buildings left as the orphans, as it were, of departed (or noticeably restructured) industries. Thus, textiles are still produced on a considerable scale in Bradford, Huddersfield and Halifax, but the industry, using up to date machines, no longer finds the buildings of the Victorian woollen industry appropriate to its needs, preferring to work in modern sheds instead. The buildings therefore require re-use.

The 'problem' industrial buildings which form the subject of this report are mills, breweries and maltings, warehouses (railway, canal and town centre), and large factories of every sort. The

21

problem is no longer one purely associated with 19th century buildings. Some massive 20th century industrial structures have now become redundant. Battersea Power Station, built (in several stages) between 1929 and 1955, is a prime example, but others include the huge Fort Dunlop rubber factory in Birmingham and the much-admired Brynmawr Rubber Factory (built 1946-53 to designs by the Architects' Co-operative Partnership) in South Wales. A number of buildings associated with the motor industry, particularly in the West Midlands, have become redundant. In all, there may be as much as 200 million sq ft of vacant industrial space in Britain.

### The Benefits of Conversion

Industrial buildings were generally 'built to last'. Durability and sturdiness were the first consideration of their builders, so that it was in the industrial field that new methods of construction – the use of iron and steel, subsequently of reinforced concrete and of light concrete construction – have been pioneered. To build a standard modern factory/warehouse shed in most parts of Britain now costs £40/£50 per sq ft. Refurbishment is inevitably better value, if the existing building can be made to work for the new user. Most large industrial buildings are extremely flexible, with very generous spaces which adapt to subdivision.

For some businesses, converted buildings do not compare well with new. Certain advanced electronics processes, for example, require a very highly serviced environment which can more readily be 'built in' to a new structure. These users are, however, in a minority. Old industrial buildings may become housing, shops, offices, museums, libraries and town halls. For, in addition to 'firmness', many possess more than a degree of 'delight'.

The 'functional tradition' found in industrial buildings by Sir James Richards, John Winter, and other historians working from a Modernist background has a basis in reality, but industrialists did not eschew decoration. Georgian mills like Masson Mill at Cromford, Derbyshire, of 1784, with its ranges of Venetian windows, Cressbrook Mill or New Mills at Wotton-under-Edge, Gloucestershire, are conscious architectural statements, as carefully, though less expertly, composed as a contemporary country house. The growing prestige of industry in the 19th century is reflected in the involvement of leading architects in factory design. Joseph Bonomi's Egyptian style Temple Mill at Leeds (1838-40) is as much a showpiece as the 1930s facades along London's Great West Road. At Saltaire, Lockwood & Mawson were

Masson Mill, Cromford,
Derbyshire. Sir Richard
Arkwright's 1783 mill is
flanked by later additions.

Page 23: New Mills,
Wotton-under-Edge . . .
and how many offices have
such good views?

Restored mills contribute to their environment as well as to the lives of their users

Marshall's Mill, Leeds:
Egyptian grandeur
unexpectedly amidst
industrial grime.

employed to clothe Sir Titus Salt's famous mill (engineered by William Fairbairn) in fashionable Italianate details. The major Leeds architect Thomas Ambler designed a factory/warehouse in the Moorish style. William Leiper of Glasgow produced an equally exotic design for the Templeton carpet factory in that city (1889). Ponton & Gough's granary on the Welsh Back in Bristol (1871-73) is one of the major examples of the secular Gothic style. It is not surprising that virtually all the buildings cited have recently come into new uses – their appeal and continuing prestige is evident.

Given the quality and appeal of such buildings, one might ask why the challenge of re-use has not been more frequently taken up. Other countries have been more responsive. In the United States, the image of industry was no less jaded than in Britain. Many of the older industrial towns of the Eastern seaboard were acutely depressed and locked into what seemed an intractable process of decline. Lowell, Massachusetts, is the most frequently quoted example of such a town. It developed (between 1825 and 1850) from a village into the second city of the state, with a major role in the American textile industry. The drift of the industry to the south began as early as the 1920s. Mill after mill closed, unemployment was general and by the 1960s the whole *raison*

*d'être* of Lowell seemed to have disappeared forever. The first response of the authorities to this catastrophic decline was to press on with redevelopment plans, tearing down redundant mills to create cheap replacements or, at worst, empty spaces. The policy did nothing to bring prosperity back to Lowell.

The revival of Lowell, now a world-famous example of urban renaissance, began in the mid '70s with a recognition of the basic quality of the town and of its place in the history of the nation. In 1978, the centre of Lowell, 137 acres including its famous 5.6 mile run of canals, was designated a National Historical Park. At this time, unemployment in the town stood at 12.6 per cent, 50 per cent above the national average. By 1984, it was 4.7 per cent, little more than half the national average. Today, Lowell is a showpiece city, with a million visitors a year – a Hilton Hotel has opened beside one of the canals. A network of museums and other visitor attractions has opened, many of them linked by a revised system of historic trams.

The foundations of Lowell's revival are rooted in a partnership between public and private investment. The Lowell Historic Preservation Commission (a federal agency) got $21.5 m from Congress in 1978 to launch its programme. But

Page 24: Templeton Carpet Factory, Glasgow. A brilliant advertisement for its wares.

25

by 1985, it was estimated that over $300 m had been invested in the town, most of it by private enterprise. The case of Market Mills, a complex of 1882-1902 with 280,000 sq ft of space, illustrates how that figure has been achieved.

Market Mills, long closed and in a poor state after a series of fires, was identified in a report of 1977 as a crucial element in the historic core of Lowell. It was suggested that a visitor centre be established there and that the remainder of the site be given over to a mixture of uses. In the event, the Lowell Historic Preservation Commission developed 42,000 sq ft of space on the ground floor with a gallery, studios, shops and visitor centre. The 'Melting Pot' food court features seven ethnic restaurants. The remainder of the building was converted by a private consortium, Market Mills Associates, into 230 housing units. The total cost of the Market Mills scheme was $14m. It has been a marked success, with open air concerts in the central court (restored by the LHPC) attracting crowds of up to 4,000 people.

Lowell's Wannalancit Mill was an even more daunting prospect for re-use, with over 400,000 sq ft of vacant space. It was bought in 1982 by developers Dobroth & Fryer, two years after its

Wannalancit Mill, Lowell, Massachusetts. Stupendous size has not inhibited re-use.

150 years of textile production had finally ended. (Wannalancit was the last operating mill in Lowell.) Within three years, it houses 14 companies with 450 employees. The big computer firm Wang is a major tenant and the entire site is a nursery of electronics-based industry. A typical example, Cadmus Computer Systems, took 1,000 sq ft for its three employees. Within six months, it has taken on a further 8,000 sq ft and 15 more employees. According to Dobroth & Fryer, the viability of the project depended on tax incentives they were able to utilise. For every dollar spent on rehabilitation, they were allowed a 25 cent tax credit . . . The conversion of the mills shows considerable *elan*. A striking two-storey atrium provides a

memorable entrance to what is now the 'Wannalancit Office and Technology Park'. Paintings and sculptures are displayed to good effect. Tourism is encouraged. One of the great turbines which powered the mill is preserved and a magazine article described the mill somewhat floridly as 'an uplifting blend of artistry and business acumen'.

A model for the involvement of local community and business interests in urban revival has been provided by the Lowell Plan, a consortium of local interests 'using private dollars to support public projects'. By 1986, it had raised $2.3m and its projects include a 'Main Street' scheme to bring back life to the old retail heart of Lowell, restoration work along the canals and educational initiatives.

Lowell is spectacular, but the spirit which has brought it back to life thrives elsewhere in urban America. Tax incentives have been a major encouragement in rehabilitation projects. In New York State, the Hudson river industrial communities of Troy, Waterford, Cohoes, Green Island and Watervliet have been linked by the Hudson Mohawk Industrial Gateway Corporation, a charitable organisation founded in 1972 to promote the retention and re-use of the region's industrial heritage. (With a remarkable range of industries, the region was very rich in historic industrial buildings.) The splendid Ogden Mill at Cohoes has, for example, been converted to house 115 apartments, private developer American Properties Team Inc being the recipient of a subvention of public funding to provide low cost units for the elderly. Paterson, New Jersey, is counted as the first planned industrial city in the USA, having been founded in the early 1790s. It became the site of a National Historic District even before Lowell and in 1977 an $11m federal Government grant was given to fund new development based on the refurbishment of redundant industrial buildings. In Providence, Rhode Island, the state's School of Design has converted a former iron works into its architectural studies building (opened 1978; cost $1.25m).

One attractive feature of the American rehabilitation scene is the willingness to take a superficially unappealing or mundane structure and make something positive of it. The old American Machine and Foundry Co plant in Brooklyn, NY, was considered an 'ugly nuisance' after its closure in 1969, but this early 20th century building was successfully converted into the Lutheran Medical Center, a 532 bed hospital. The cost of over $42m was estimated to be some $10m less than an entirely new hospital of equivalent size.

The Market Mills at Lowell, before and after conversion. Shops, studios and 230 apartments have been created by a private consortium.

France's record of re-using fine industrial buildings is unrivalled in Europe. In the textile towns of the north, there are industrial landscapes reminiscent of northern England and of Lancashire in particular. Lille is a striking example of revival, with major public and private funding both at work. The massive Le Blan mill was begun in 1900 and extended twice (in 1925 and 1930). It is a typical large industrial building of its age, steel framed and clad in red brick. Le Blan has been recycled by architects Reichen & Robert to become virtually a self-contained community, with 100 rented flats, shops, a small area of offices, a church, library and car park. The architects say that one of their objectives was 'to modify fundamentally the appearance of the old factory, in order to create a new image in keeping with a multi-purpose building'. The way this has been done exemplifies the bold approach of many French conversions. In places, the floors have been cut back, leaving the steel framework exposed, to create open terraces and bring light into the building. Elsewhere, great sections have been cut vertically through the mill, for example, to provide for the lofty entrance hall which gives access to the public spaces. The new identity of the mill has been emphasised by the use of paint, for instance on columns and beams. Reichen & Robert were also responsible for the conversion of the Blin & Blin Mill at Elbeuf, nearly 200,000 sq ft of space in handsome blocks dating from the 1870s. Located close to the centre of the town, the mill has been much extended and some of its best features hidden by later accretions. The aim of the architects was to rescue the building from these accretions and to reveal the elegance of its original design. Again, the principal element is rented housing (151 units), with a smaller area of shops, offices and workshops plus parking. The courtyard in the midst of the site is an attractive feature. At Tourcoing, Reichen & Robert were responsible for the conversion of the Prouvost Mill into 162 flats plus 60,000 sq ft of offices.

Back in Lille, a great deal has been achieved by the entrepreneur David Avital, promoter of the 'Tertiaries'. Avital has now completed six conversion schemes in the city, totalling 500,000 sq ft, and is engaged in several more. His first project involved the conversion of the former Declercq factory into offices and housing. Tertiare II (completed 1981) was a conversion of another Le Blan mill, 75,000 sq ft in area, into offices. An internal courtyard has been scooped out of the centre of the building to provide natural light. The space available was oversubscribed before conversion work was completed. Tertiare VI, recently completed, took the far larger (200,000 sq ft) Wallaerts Mill (1898-1906) and made of it offices, a regional training college

(30,000 sq ft) and some flats. The architectural treatment is again bold, with sections of the mill cut back to the steel frame to provide light wells, a striking internal atrium, new fenestration and quite extensive rebuilding of whole sections to give the structure a new image. The porch made up of columns taken from the atrium area is a witty addition. A large part of the mill has been taken by the Phillips Telephone Company, but small units (under 2,000 sq ft) are available. There is, it seems, relatively little demand for small workshop units in Lille, but Avital's projects have attracted large firms and Government agencies as tenants. In eight years, he has become a major figure in Lille, a champion of what he described as 'le lifting urbain'. He believes that refurbished buildings have a strong appeal of their own: 'Brick buildings have warmth . . . they are solid and provide a feeling of

security. People like working in them. The stability of our tenants is proof in itself!' Whilst deeply rooted in the region, which has half the vacant industrial space in the country, Avital is now looking at possible developments throughout France.

France is a politically centralised nation, with an enduring tradition of high levels of public subsidy for cultural and 'heritage' projects. In and around Paris, 'les grands projets' promoted by successive Presidents have included major rehabilitation schemes. The most notable is the Musée d'Orsay, housed in the former railway station of the same name. Architect Gae Aulenti's adaptation of the carefully restored trainshed is controversial and contrasts with the lightness of touch which Reichen & Robert have shown in their adaptation of the Halle des Boeufs at La Villette (the former Paris abattoir complex) as a vast

Tertiare II, Lille, France. A mill converted into offices by a local entrepreneur who has made a speciality of converting industrial buildings.

(300,000 sq ft) exhibition hall. This great building, 60 feet high and over 750 feet long, has been most elegantly converted and new insertions, whilst distinctly 'of their age', are in sympathy with the character of the original structure. The cost of the scheme was FF145m (FF5,000 per square metre), a sum which compared very favourably with that of a new structure of similar size.

By far the largest building at La Villette (a 136 acre site) is the 1960s abattoir building, now the Centre for Science & Industry. This colossal block, almost 1.5m sq ft in size, has been spectacularly converted (architect: Adrien Fainsilber) to house one of the finest science museums in the world. With a towering internal atrium as its central feature, the Centre (which opened in March, 1986) cost FF4.5 billion to establish.

Stylish and imaginative conversions of industrial buildings are to be found throughout France. In Nantes, the 1850s Le Manu tobacco factory (closed in 1974, when operations were transferred to an out-of-town industrial park) was converted to flats, a library, creche, public hall, shops and restaurant. The wool exchange at Bordeaux (C Deschamps, 1822-24) has become a cultural centre. The Royal Rope Factory at Rochefort (1666-1670) has become offices for Government agencies and the base of the local chamber of commerce.

Industrial buildings have been the subject of outstanding conversion schemes throughout Europe. The Grain Warehouse in Limerick, Ireland (now housing a wide variety of uses), the brewery at Kalmer, Sweden, now flats, and the fine grain warehouse in Copenhagen (now the 366 bed Admiral Hotel) are examples. The Admiral Hotel is just one of a magnificent run of late 18th century warehouses on the city's waterfront, and all the remainder have become flats.

### Britain Gets the Message
The 'recycling' of industrial buildings is, in a sense, a process which has been going on in Britain for a very long time. Well-built structures intended for one industrial use can readily adapt to another. In the textile towns of West Yorkshire and Greater Manchester, mills which have gone out of production have often been colonised by an army of small enterprises. *Mills in the 80s*, a report commissioned in 1984 by the former Greater Manchester and West Yorkshire County Councils, found a staggering 30 million sq ft of vacant industrial space in the two counties. But it also found that 'the economics of occupying old industrial buildings are a fundamental feature of

Fiat's Lingotto plant in Turin, built in 1923 as a factory of the future, is being converted into an ambitious business and cultural centre.

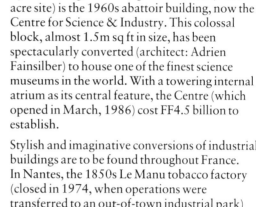

The exterior of the Lingotto building following restoration.

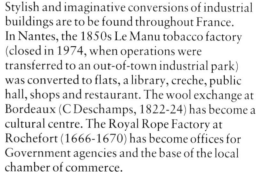

Accommodation provided in the restored factory.

Dryden Street, Covent Garden, London. A working community for design professionals.

Barley Mow Workspace, Chiswick, London . . . backed by Cornhill Insurance.

their attractiveness. For the purchaser, they can be acquired for between £1 and £2 per sq ft in the case of good quality multi-storey premises and for £3-£5 per sq ft in the case of single storey buildings. This compares with £18-£22 per sq ft for new premises'. These figures now need to be updated, but the comparative advantages of conversion remain. Buildings could be rented (1984 levels) at as little as 80p per sq ft The report recognised the value of this reservoir of cheap space to the regional economy. Some 80-85 per cent of re-used space went to manufacturing industry, warehousing and repairing operations. Some could only remain viable if able to secure cheap accommodation. Some 'bad neighbour' uses (for example, vehicle repairers) were best located in industrial areas. Demand for small units in old industrial buildings was likely, the report concluded, to remain strong. The problems associated with re-used buildings were not, however, to be underestimated: the poor state of some buildings and the unwillingness or inability of small businesses to fund repairs, their inadequate layout for many modern needs and the lack of modern services – lifts, lavatories, parking – which employees now expect. It was likely that firms wishing to improve their 'image' would move to new premises when they could afford to. In other words, old buildings were rated as second-best.

Ironically enough, the growing trend towards the refurbishment of our older industrial buildings has coincided with the rapid contraction or restructuring of most of the industries which produced them. Increasingly, the Industrial Revolution recedes into history and its impedimenta – steam engines, heavy machinery, engineering structures, workers' houses and mills – acquire the patina of antiquity.

The earliest conscious 'conversions' of industrial buildings in Britain took place away from the industrial heartlands and involved buildings of relatively modest size. During the 1970s, it had been gradually realised that one of the drawbacks of comprehensive redevelopment (then coming under increasing criticism) was the loss of employment brought about by the destruction of small industrial premises. At the same time, the large traditional industries were in decline. Between 1960 and 1978, for example, manufacturing employment in Britain's large cities fell by 27 per cent – in London the figure was 43 per cent. (An URBED survey, 1977, found 1.5m sq ft of vacant space between Waterloo and London Bridge!) The importance of small businesses became even more apparent. In 1960, few politicians cared about them. By 1975, their survival was a matter of national interest.

Ransome's Dock, Battersea, London. A derelict cold store transformed by windows and a new skyline.

The 'working community' at 5 Dryden Street, London, was formed (by architects Rock Townsend) as early as 1972, primarily to accommodate 'design' based professionals. Clerkenwell Workshops, in contrast, was established in 1976 in two disused warehouses with a total floor area of 59,000 sq ft, the aim being to provide accommodation for traditional local industries including jewellery manufacture. The specially formed company which carried out the project began with only £1,000 capital. By 1981, 130 units there employed over 350 people. At Barley Mow Workspace, housed in CFA Voysey's wallpaper factory in Chiswick, the promoters persuaded a major institution, Cornhill Insurance, to put up funds for conversion. Workspaces of this sort have now become a patently sound investment and developments of this sort are common throughout inner London and in the major provincial cities. The basis of working communities is that there are some shared services (for example, switchboard/reception and conference rooms) and, in many cases, an interaction of the tenants. For instance, architects may find it convenient to have a quantity surveyor in the same building. In some areas, the communities may be based on one industry (for example, in the Jewellery Quarter, Birmingham). Workspace type developments have now become – in some locations, at least – thoroughly commercial but some have had to be supported, to meet local needs, by grant aid, chiefly Urban Development Grant. The conversion of the Argent Works in Birmingham, costing £490,000, got a grant of £151,000.

## New Style Developers

Dr Nicholas Falk of URBED (which played an important part in the working communities movement) wrote in 1985: 'We need to encourage new kinds of developers, able to take on complex and long term programmes with social and economic, as well as physical, goals . . . we need a new breed of 'social entrepreneur' . . . There is some evidence that 'social entrepreneurs' are now emerging in Britain.

Hull is one of Britain's most under-valued cities and its Old Town, in particular, deteriorated after the war (when it suffered serious damage from bombing) into a depressing backwater. However, the Old Town, close to the docks, contains a fascinating mixture of buildings of all periods. Francis Daly and Ben Hooson have been pioneers in bringing back the life of the area. Daly, an engineer by training, took a long lease on two warehouses on Prince's Dock (dating from 1830 and 1860 and listed Grade II) from the local authority. He has converted them into the Waterfront Hotel and a nightclub. Daly used neither architect nor contractor, personally designing and supervising the conversion of the buildings, and received only a limited amount of grant aid (from the local authority and the Historic Buildings Council). One pleasing feature is the retention of much of the internal timber structures – this involved hard bargaining with the fire officers. The scheme has given Hull a very useful new amenity.

Ben Hooson is another new-style Hull developer. The Pease warehouse on the river Hull, dating in part from the 1740s, had been written off as beyond economic repair by the City Council and seemed doomed to demolition. Hooson acquired the building and, as Phase I of his overall scheme for the site, converted it into 18 flats for sale. HBC grant helped to make the conversion viable and most of the timber interior had to be sacrificed in the development. But the Pease scheme, now complete, had a major impact on the Old Town, confirming its attractiveness as a place to live. Other developers have since moved in. The Merchants' Warehouse on Market Square has, for example, been converted into 28 flats by North British Urban Renewal Ltd.

The South Pennine region between Manchester and Leeds is now often cited as an example of striking revival. One of its great assets is the existence of fine – indeed, spectacular – country close to its large towns. But it has been a prime industrial area for 150 years, and even in the country mills are a part of the landscape. The decline of employment in textiles hit many towns hard. Hebden Bridge, some ten miles west of

The pioneering conversion of the Pease Warehouse in Hull into apartments showed that the Old Town could be an attractive place to live.

# In Hull, waterfront warehouses have been the key to a commercial success story

The Waterfront Hotel and Nightclub created in a disused warehouse on Prince's Dock by a local entrepreneur.

The reception area and roof-garden restaurant, before and after conversion.

Dean Clough Mills, Halifax. Crossley's vast textile mills appeared a lost cause when the Company moved out in 1983. However, the vision and energy of Ernest Hall has made it one of the most successful small business centres in Britain – and now major insurance companies and even the local VAT office have moved in.

Halifax, drifted into acute depression during the 1960s, so that up to half the shops in the town were empty and there seemed to be no interest in investing there. It was fortunate to have a group of residents who cared enough about its future to invest both money and time in its revival. David Fletcher, a lecturer, turned entrepreneur when he bought the redundant Bridge Mill at the centre of the town and successfully turned it into craft workshops, a restaurant and shops. The Bridge Mill project was a major breakthrough in perceptions of the town's future prospects. There were, however, other buildings in the town and region at risk and Pennine Heritage, a registered charity, was established by Fletcher and others in 1979 to promote investment and revival. One of its major achievements has been the conversion of the Nutclough Mill at Hebden Bridge, long empty, into craft and light industrial workshops.

Without doubt the most spectacular example of re-use in this region – and one of national significance – is to be found at Dean Clough Mills in Halifax. Dean Clough, which produced carpets, grew from small beginnings to be the town's largest employer. By 1860 it covered 18 acres and employed 5,000 people. The present buildings, filling the valley bottom just west of the town centre, range in date from the 1840s to the 1860s and amount to around 1.25 million sq ft of space. A high proportion of this is in the multi-storey blocks. In the present century, the company passed out of the hands of the founding Crossley dynasty and was eventually swallowed up by the mammoth Carpets International

conglomerate. Under their management, the scale of operations at Dean Clough was steadily reduced and in 1983 the mills were completely closed. This was seen as a body blow to the town, since several hundred jobs were lost.

Dean Clough now houses over 200 small firms with a total workforce of almost 1,500. Under the inspired direction of Ernest Hall, it has become the Dean Clough Industrial Park. Well over half of the total space there is occupied by businesses which range from car repairing to printing, computer sales and design companies. Dean Clough also plays a major part in fostering the growth of new businesses in the region. The Calderdale Business Innovation Centre, based there, is 50:50 private/public funded and includes a computer training centre. The site boasts several eating places, an art gallery and conference facilities. A sculpture park is planned on waste ground adjacent to the mills. Only one major building has been demolished – a multi-storey block removed to open up the congested core of the site.

Dean Clough is a personal triumph for Ernest Hall, whose involvement in the running of the project is very close. No government money was given (or sought) to fund the acquisition and conversion of the buildings. In fact, 'conversion' is not really an appropriate term. The buildings have generally proved very suitable for the needs of the new users and works have been limited to repainting, new electrics and plumbing and the insertion of partitioning to create individual workspaces.

Ferguslie No 1 Mill in Scotland has been the subject of two applications to demolish – the mill stands empty and deteriorating

Ferguslie No 1 Spinning Mill, Paisley.

Tobacco Warehouse, Stanley Dock, Liverpool. Completed in 1900, this vast, spectacular warehouse contains over one million square feet of floor space in search of a new use.

## Future Possibilities

What has been achieved in Britain in terms of conversion and re-use so far is extremely encouraging, but the potential remains enormous.

The Lancashire cotton town of Burnley (the subject of SAVE's report *Mill Town Image: Burden or Asset?*) exemplifies this potential. A century ago it was the greatest cotton weaving town in Europe, with 100,000 looms, but very little cotton now passes through Burnley. During the last quarter of a century, efforts have been made to erase the town's industrial past, but more recently there has been something of a change of heart. The so-called 'Weavers triangle' along the Leeds-Liverpool Canal has been widely recognised as the central element in the town's industrial heritage. Yet a number of buildings here stand empty still. (Tragically, the best, Clocktower Mill of the 1940s, has recently been destroyed by fire). One of the best (and relatively few) surviving mills in nearby Rawtenstall, Ilex, has been standing empty and neglected for years and is threatened with demolition. In Bradford, Manningham Mills, the city's most prominent industrial monument, is vacant above ground floor level and in an increasingly poor condition. Bradford has an abundance of empty or half-empty mills, and in 'Little Germany', the warehouse district close to the city centre, there is similarly a great deal of vacant space.

Scotland reflects the same picture. The listed Ferguslie No 1 Mill in Paisley (built in 1886 and 272,000 sq ft in area) has been the subject of two applications to demolish. The second was rejected by the Secretary of State for Scotland in December 1987, on the grounds that there was little evidence of serious efforts to find a new use for the mill. But the mill still stands empty and deteriorating. At the heart of Glasgow stand a series of outstanding but unused (or underused) industrial buildings.

The Broomielaw district of Glasgow, along the banks of the Clyde, contains some of the best of these buildings, including the massive tobacco bonds on James Watt Street. But redevelopment plans for this area would retain only a few of them and the emphasis is on new buildings, not conversion.

Too often, the potential of redundant industrial buildings is only half-realised in second-rate and unimaginative conversion schemes. This is especially apparent in London's Docklands. Two of the pioneering schemes here, New Concordia Wharf and Thames Tunnel Mills, remain amongst the best. Andrew Wadsworth bought the warehouse buildings at New Concordia Wharf in 1979 and, with architects Pollard, Thomas, Edwards, converted them profitably into 60 flats, 20,000 sq ft of workshops/studios and a smaller area of offices. The internal structure of the warehouses was retained, load-bearing wooden floors being covered in concrete decks. Externally, the two dominant features were preserved – a massive water-tower which Piers Gough converted into a luxurious penthouse, and the chimney, which it had formerly been proposed to pull down. The riverside balconies of the flats, made of cast iron and nautical in flavour, actually enhance the building. Thames Tunnel Mills, converted by Hunt Thompson for the London & Quadrant Housing Trust, is a flour mill of the 1880s. The most striking feature of the conversion (to 71 rented flats) is the new atrium, rising a full six storeys inside the building.

In comparison with these schemes, the conversions of the Gun Wharves in Wapping by Barratt Homes is harsh and lacking in imagination – standard modern windows and concrete lintels are jarring intrusions. (As much might be said of some of the Barratt schemes in Leith – for example, 'Maritime Court', where the interiors retain no trace of their original character and the exteriors also have been largely recast). Work of this kind is all too common – a waste of the rich and unique potential of historic buildings.

The conversion of handsome warehouses and mills to new uses is now far from uncommon: the image of these buildings is now generally seen as positive. The success of prestigious schemes in London Docklands and elsewhere is likely to further enhance this image. However, there are many industrial buildings of immense value whose merits are largely unrecognized. In particular, those of the present century are virtually undiscovered. The Brynmawr Rubber Factory in South Wales is a good example.

The factory was built in 1946-52 to designs by the Architects' Co-operative Partnership, itself a newly founded practice of high Modernist ideals. The *Architectural Review* said of the architects' achievement: 'They have created not only a good factory, but an idea for a factory'. The idea – revolutionary in the late '40s – was to avoid 'The Great West Road approach', the factory disguised beneath a veneer of styling. Central to ACP's concept was a new relationship between workers and managers – all entered by a common ramped approach and shared one canteen and other communal facilities. The centre of the factory was a great (77,000 sq ft) production area covered by nine shell concrete domes, using a technology new to Britain, the aim being to create

Thames Tunnel Mills, Rotherhithe, London, converted for a housing trust.

At Thames Tunnel Mills a large internal atrium has been created to bring daylight into the centre of the building.

Page 39: New Concordia Wharf, Bermondsey, London. Now some of the most sought-after apartments in Docklands.

a huge area of uncluttered floor space. The factory (according to John Summerson 'One of the few British industrial buildings of this century which deserves to be called a classic') was closed in 1981 and since then has been listed Grade II* (a due recognition of its qualities). Despite the efforts of a working party and of the local authority, no use has yet been found for it.

There is surely a case for the 'mothballing' of buildings of this quality which have no immediate use and yet need not be demolished. An example of the futility of demolition can be seen in Hull, where the Railway Dock warehouses – a splendid run – were pulled down as useless during the 1970s. Had they survived, there can be no doubt that developers would now be competing to acquire them. Industrial buildings are extremely well-constructed and can usually tolerate long periods of disuse and neglect with minimal maintenance. At Stanley Dock in Liverpool, the colossal 1900 tobacco warehouse – perhaps the largest single building in the city – is currently seen simply as a problem building. Yet 10 years ago, there appeared to be no use for the splendid Albert Dock buildings. Now they are one of the prime sights of the North. The moral is clear.

By their very nature, industrial buildings, particularly of the 20th century, adapt to radical remodelling – where it is appropriate. Terry Farrell's TV/am and Limehouse Studios schemes are essentially economical remodellings on existing concrete frames. At TV/am, a redundant two storey garage provided the raw material for a building intended to project the image of the clients in a memorable fashion. This approach to 'recycling' buildings is common in the USA and has more to do with common-sense attitudes to the proper use of resources than with aesthetics.

The industrial heritage is never far from sight in Britain and it is gradually being realised that industrial architecture is, indeed, a part of our patrimony as much as castles or cathedrals or Georgian squares. We have not yet come to terms with the problems of re-use which it sometimes poses, but there is every prospect that the industrial past will increasingly become a part of our future.

With imagination and enterprise look what can be done – owners pay a premium
for the character of these desirable flats

# Candidates for Conversion

2

**Hunslet Mill, Leeds**
**Friargate Warehouse, Derby**
**Calder and Hebble Navigation**
**Warehouse, Wakefield**
**Cressbrook Mill, Derbyshire**
**The Tannery, London**
Proposals by Francis Machin RIBA

Detail from a proposal for
the Calder and Hebble
Navigation Warehouse,
Wakefield.

All the walls on the first and second floors of this building have been drilled for dynamite

## Hunslet Mill, Leeds

Today Hunslet Mill and its surrounding wasteland is a symbol of inner city dereliction. These proposals show how, with vision and imagination, it could become a flagship of urban regeneration. Situated close to the end of the M1 motorway it has better communications than the city centre.

A massive amount of clearance has already taken place – increasing the sense of desolation. The demolition of Hunslet Mill would complete the clean-sweep: here we suggest how its preservation and re-use can provide the element of continuity essential in a great city, and set a scale for the whole district.

Filled with new low buildings the area will never have the presence it had in Victorian times. The retention of this major landmark building will give Hunslet an immediate identity.

This is flat, low lying land – a new tower, scaled to Hunslet Mill, will create a new image. For all the dereliction, the area has one major plus – magnificent views over the River Aire – high buildings can take advantage of this in a way low ones cannot.

The need is to create a sense of excitement on the approach, an excitement that is maintained as you park your car, and arrive at the main entrance. There is abundant space for car parking – this needs to be laid out under avenues of trees, on a strict geometrical plan, responding to the strong, simple lines of the old mill.

The attraction of Hunslet Mill today is that it has the high ceilings essential for modern offices. The elevations illustrated here show that it has precisely the attributes of a large modern office block – long rows of evenly spaced, identical windows, providing good, natural lighting for the large open spaces within.

Only one major new element is necessary – a new vertical access tower, providing an imposing – and eyecatching – entrance, with good lifts and staircases. The perspectives here show that the drama and appeal of the canal can be increased by other large buildings along the water – responding in style and scale to Hunslet Mill. The site is large enough to accept high density along the canal. The solution therefore depends on bold landscaping and exciting new buildings as well as refurbishment of Hunslet Mill. Together they will transform the prospects of this whole section of the city.

Hunslet Mill was built in 1838-40 for steam-powered flax spinning. Its design has been reliably attributed to the great engineer William Fairbairn, and is close in construction technique to his Orell's Mill at Stockport (1834, now

Hunslet Mill, Leeds. The staircase tower encloses an impressive stone spiral stair rising the height of the building.

demolished). The main block is a good example of pioneering fireproof construction, with cast-iron columns, supporting cast-iron beams and brick arched ceilings.

During the 1840s and 1850s extensive warehouses and a new boiler house were added. Most of these have now been swept away. Demolition of the main mill has been delayed by listing. (It is now Grade II* in recognition of its pioneering structural design).

A feasibility study by Derek Latham and Associates has highlighted the problem of straightforward refurbishment. In 1986 the cost of basic repair was estimated at £0.5m. Costings for conversion to light industrial use was estimated at £1.25m and for offices at £3m. Surveyors estimated that likely rent levels would not be high enough to make the operation commercially viable.

Hence the present proposals for improving the character of the whole surrounding area and for injecting a major element of exciting new architecture.

Page 42: Hunslet Mill, Leeds, reflected in the River Aire, overlooks a wilderness of derelict railway yards.

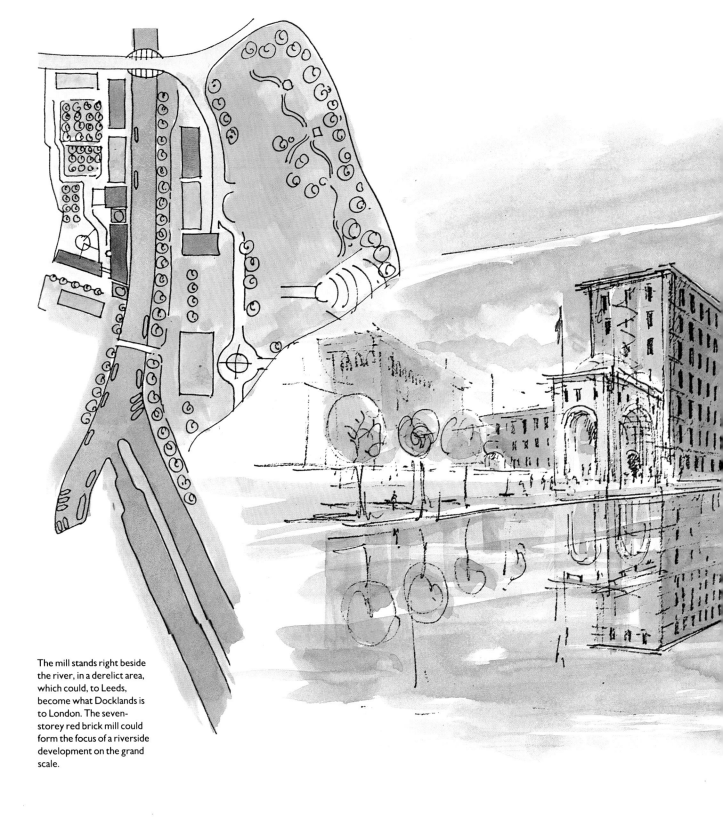

The mill stands right beside the river, in a derelict area, which could, to Leeds, become what Docklands is to London. The seven-storey red brick mill could form the focus of a riverside development on the grand scale.

Hunslet Mill and the River Aire become the focal point of a new, landscaped business park.

Leeds station

River Aire

M1

Hunslet Mill

The mill is close to the city centre, the railway station and the M1.

**Impressive and attractively landscaped car parking . . . such opportunities are rare in the inner city.**

There is a need to create a sense of arrival, which could be achieved by planting avenues of trees, and terminating the existing road in a strong architectural feature which would form the entrance foyer.

The strong character of Hunslet Mill provides a foil for large new buildings in various differing styles. The canalised river provides a flat reflective surface which is a rare opportunity for both buildings and landscaping.

There is ample space to be able to provide elegantly landscaped car parking between rows of trees, with sculptures and fountains. Maximum site development can be achieved by creating tall buildings, which would also help to identify the site from a distance. It is important to preserve views through to the river from the various courtyards and approach roads.

The adjacent wasteland should be generously planted with trees to create a true urban parkland surrounding the new buildings.

# The elegance of simplicity combined with large amounts of flexible space

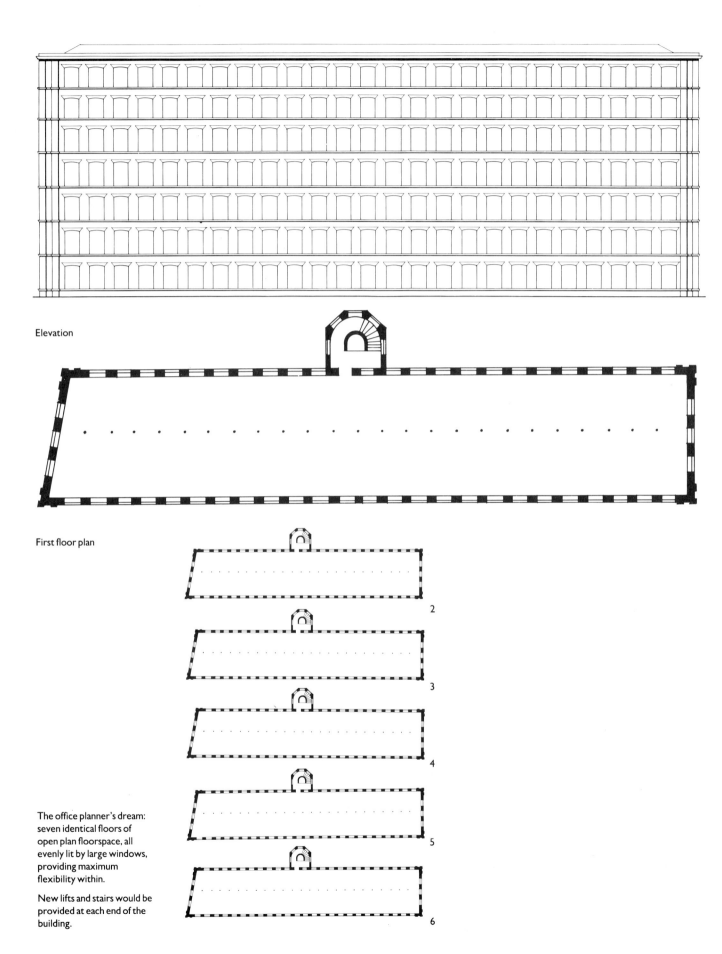

Elevation

First floor plan

2

3

4

5

6

The office planner's dream:
seven identical floors of
open plan floorspace, all
evenly lit by large windows,
providing maximum
flexibility within.

New lifts and stairs would be
provided at each end of the
building.

48

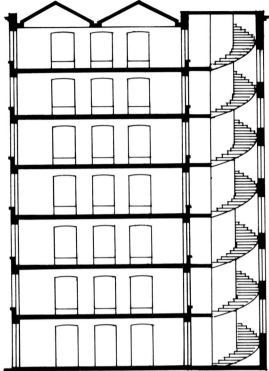

Transverse section

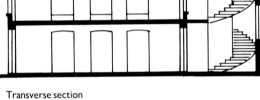

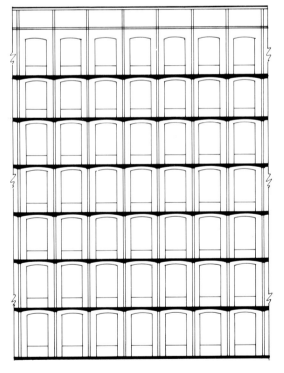

Longitudinal section

The main approach leads straight up to an eyecatching new entrance atrium, tall enough to contain mature trees.

The ample dimensions of each floor provide space for the creation of self-contained offices on either side of a large expanse of open plan layout.

The view is framed by well-proportioned windows, comparable in size to those in new office blocks. The brick arch vaults could be retained – with lighting and services carried on an exposed track system.

Hunslet Mill is the only remaining building of architectural merit in an abandoned, urban wilderness where recent development has contributed nothing to the quality of the environment.

E

Utilitarian sheds are no substitute for the noble proportions of the Victorian mill. The tragedy is that so far the only new buildings in the area are wholly undistinguished.

F

Left: Italianate detail emphasises the engine room.

Right: Elegantly proportioned windows give style to an enormous goods shed.

## Friargate Warehouse, Derby

Imagine shopping in Harrods with Versailles for a car park. Formal landscaping, we suggest, could be the key to a really imaginative and stylish re-use of this handsome Victorian railway warehouse. A strong axial approach can be created, following the line of the old railway tracks which entered the building head-on.

A large amount of former railway land surrounds the building, providing space for extensive areas of surface car parking – an essential for every major shopping centre. The building also has the virtue of being very close to the centre of Derby.

To make the most of the approach, a central pedestrian alley, flanked by trees, is proposed. The car parking, screened by planting, is laid out symmetrically on either side.

The internal layout of the building makes it particularly appropriate for conversion as a shopping mall. It is arranged on three levels: a basement, with road access, which is suitable for servicing and deliveries; the ground floor, where the railway tracks entered, which becomes the main shopping mall; and a first floor storage area, which can be adapted as an upper level of shopping.

The internal structure consists of cast iron columns, carrying wrought iron beams and wooden floors. The very high ground floor could be adapted to take a mezzanine, offering three levels of shopping, if required. The existing floor area is 11,080 square metres.

Anyone moving into a building such as this is likely to want to give it a strong, fresh identity. This could be achieved by simple additions to the main front – a canopy, a pediment, or at simplest just a group of flagpoles. For the rest the warehouse takes its character from the excellent brickwork, with economic but effective decoration in the form of pilasters and corbelling.

The Friargate Warehouse was the product of the Great Northern Railway Company's efforts to infiltrate the territory of the omnipotent Midland Railway which had its headquarters at Derby. It was built in 1877-78 to the designs of Kirk and Randall of Sleaford. A passenger station was planned but never built, and the warehouse reflects the predominance of goods traffic on the GNR.

It remained in railway use until 1971; subsequently it was let to a range of small businesses. In 1985 a locally-based firm, C W Clowes (Investments) Ltd obtained planning permission for a £6 m comprehensive development of the site, including a sports complex, DIY store, garden centre, housing and car parking.

There was, however, strong opposition to the proposed demolition of the GNR warehouse, from both the Derbyshire Archaeological Society and the Derby Civic Society, and in 1986 the warehouse and the adjoining hydraulic engine shed were both listed Grade II. Meanwhile, a plan to extend the Derby inner ring road has put a blight on this area of the city. However, there is no financial provision for it in the county's road construction programme over the next ten years, and a minor realignment would spare the listed buildings and most of the site.

The hydraulic engine house, built of red and blue brick, with an attractive Italianate tower, could be restored as an added attraction for family visits. The extensive area of former railway land would also be highly suitable for a garden centre.

As well as a shopping and leisure complex on the GNR warehouse, we also illustrate a scheme for converting the warehouse as a multi-storey car park. A short minibus/ferry service could take people in to the city centre – eliminating the need for multi-storey car parks in the city centre itself.

Page 52: Friargate Warehouse, Derby. An example of masterful brickwork from the height of the railway age.

The warehouse is in easy reach of the proposed southern ring road, as well as the city centre – perfect for a modern shopping centre. Road access for shoppers and delivery vehicles is excellent, while disused railway land could provide an attractive pedestrian link to the city centre.

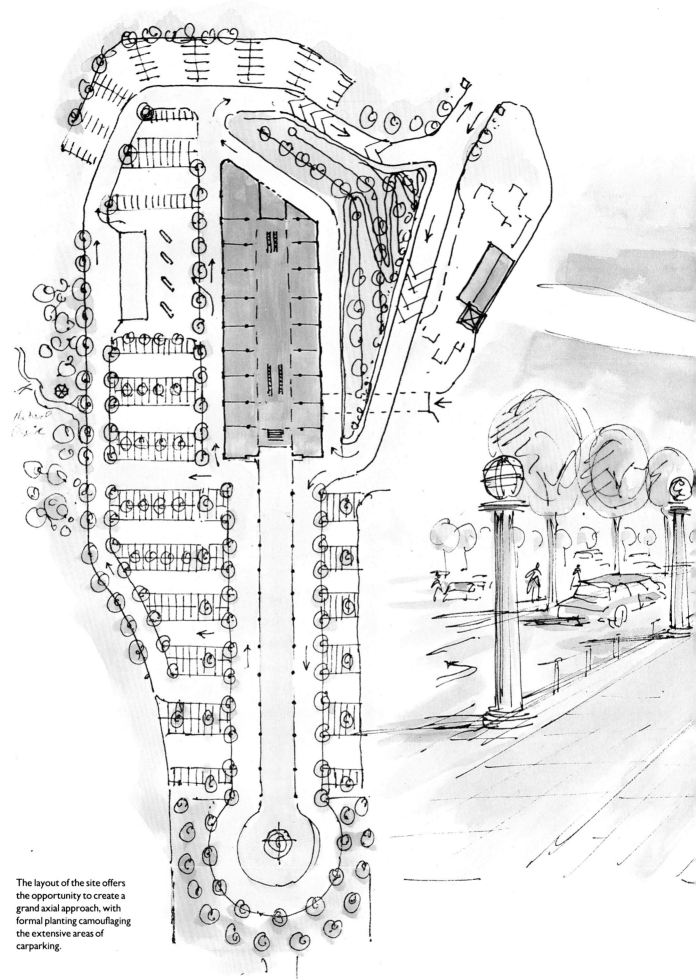

The layout of the site offers
the opportunity to create a
grand axial approach, with
formal planting camouflaging
the extensive areas of
carparking.

Imagine shopping at Harrods with Versailles for a car park

This building adapts excellently as a shopping mall on three levels

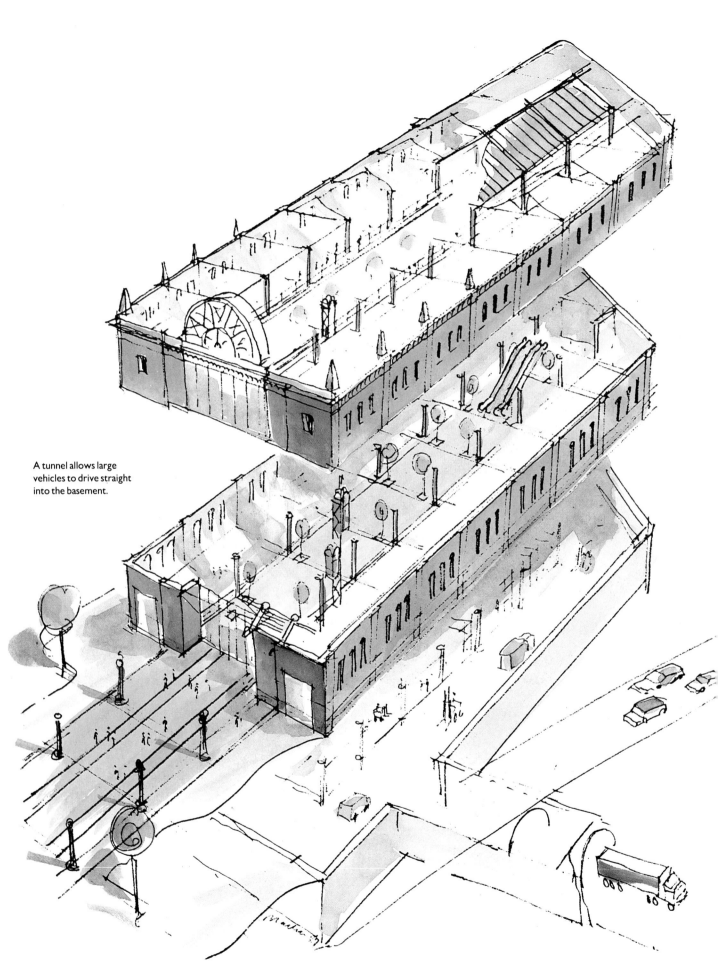

A tunnel allows large
vehicles to drive straight
into the basement.

# Six ways of adding a flourish to the front

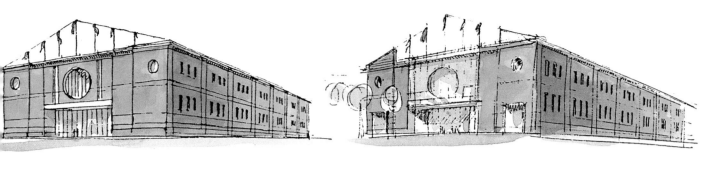

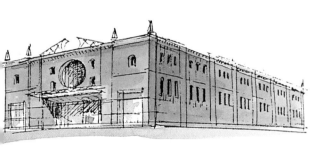

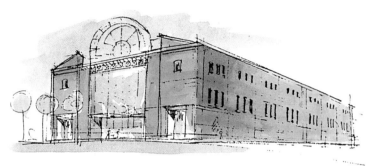

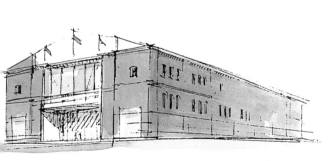

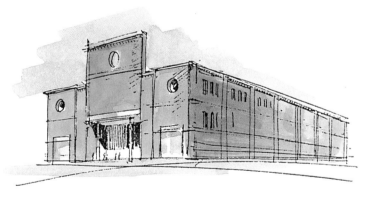

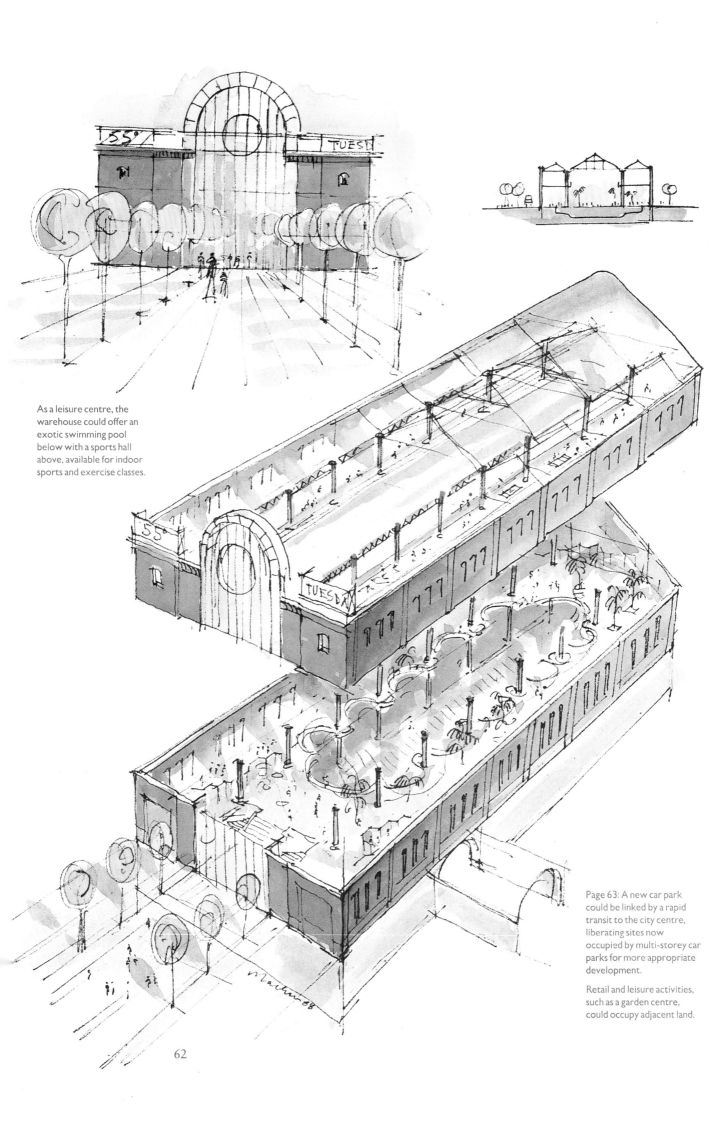

As a leisure centre, the warehouse could offer an exotic swimming pool below with a sports hall above, available for indoor sports and exercise classes.

Page 63: A new car park could be linked by a rapid transit to the city centre, liberating sites now occupied by multi-storey car parks for more appropriate development.

Retail and leisure activities, such as a garden centre, could occupy adjacent land.

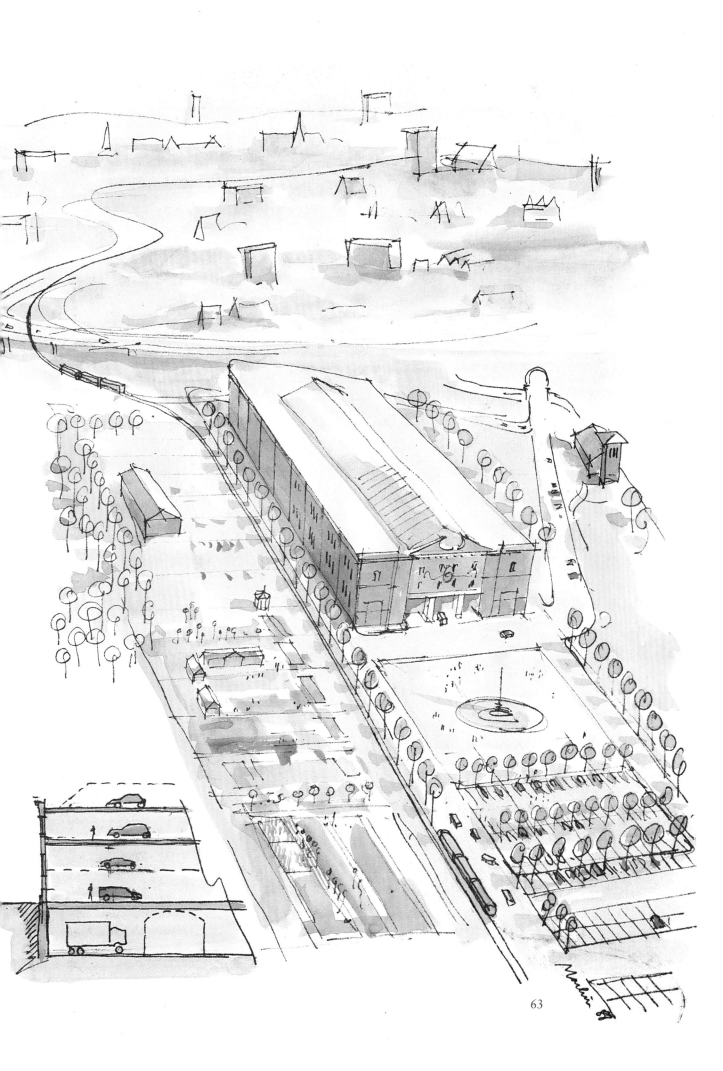

63

## Calder and Hebble Navigation Warehouse, Wakefield

This is a handsome riverside warehouse, by no means intimidatingly large, which has been blighted by careless treatment of its surroundings. The waterfront at Wakefield should be one of the town's most attractive features – with the river and weir curling through the town centre in a great sweep. Blight has come in the form of a new road cutting unsympathetically across the river, overshadowing the town's medieval bridge, remarkable for its mid-river chapel. As a result this warehouse and neighbouring buildings have been left in an isolated pocket.

The plusses nonetheless potentially outweigh the drawbacks. A site on the water's edge provides fine views, and careful landscaping of the immediate surroundings can create an attractive enclave, screened from local industry and traffic.

Various uses have been considered – including a hotel and a restaurant; the problem is that the building is out of the way for such uses, and the wider context is not yet appealing – though as other buildings are restored on both sides of the river, property alongside will be more in demand.

The proposal illustrated here is for a business centre aimed at new companies and young people starting up on their own. Accommodation would be provided on an easy-come, easy-go basis.

Central facilities would be provided – security, reception, secretarial services, conference rooms and catering.

For businesses such as these there is a special attraction in having an office in an unusual and interesting building. Warehouses, in particular, are very much in vogue for this purpose. New work and finishes can be stylish and colourful – though the basic warehouse character – cast-iron columns, exposed walls and timbers – will remain.

The building is soundly constructed of stone, with a stone slate roof – and provides some 400 square metres, gross, floor area. Lighting could be brought into the centre of the building by the introduction of a glass-roofed atrium.

One of the attractions of an 'innovation' centre such as this is that it does not matter if the immediate environs are scruffy and the approach awkward – so long as there is a 'buzz' apparent on arrival, and the building itself looks lively and interesting.

The adjoining dock, which is used as a marina, provides a further special attraction and could be the focus for further development with new buildings of eye-catching design. The dock provides the link which by-passes the weir, and will become increasingly lively and attractive as river traffic increases.

The dock alongside has potential as a focal point for sympathetic new development.

Page 64: It is typical of early canal warehouses, with an internal loading dock from which goods could be lifted straight out of the barge.

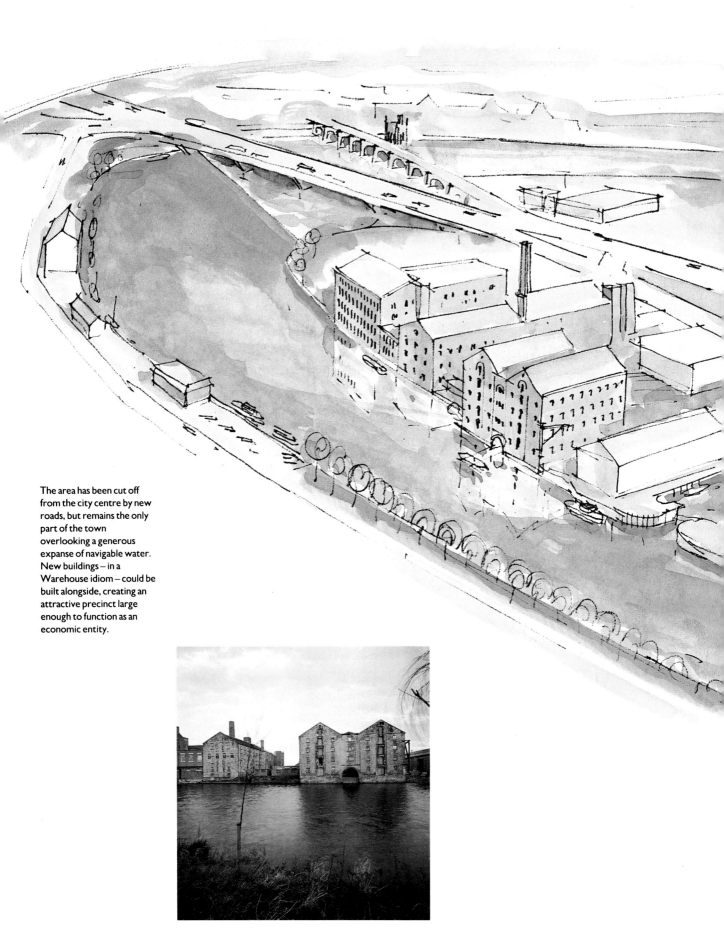

The area has been cut off from the city centre by new roads, but remains the only part of the town overlooking a generous expanse of navigable water. New buildings – in a Warehouse idiom – could be built alongside, creating an attractive precinct large enough to function as an economic entity.

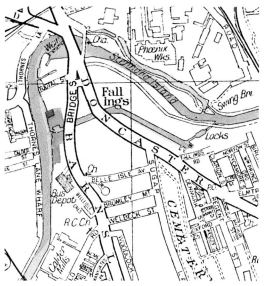

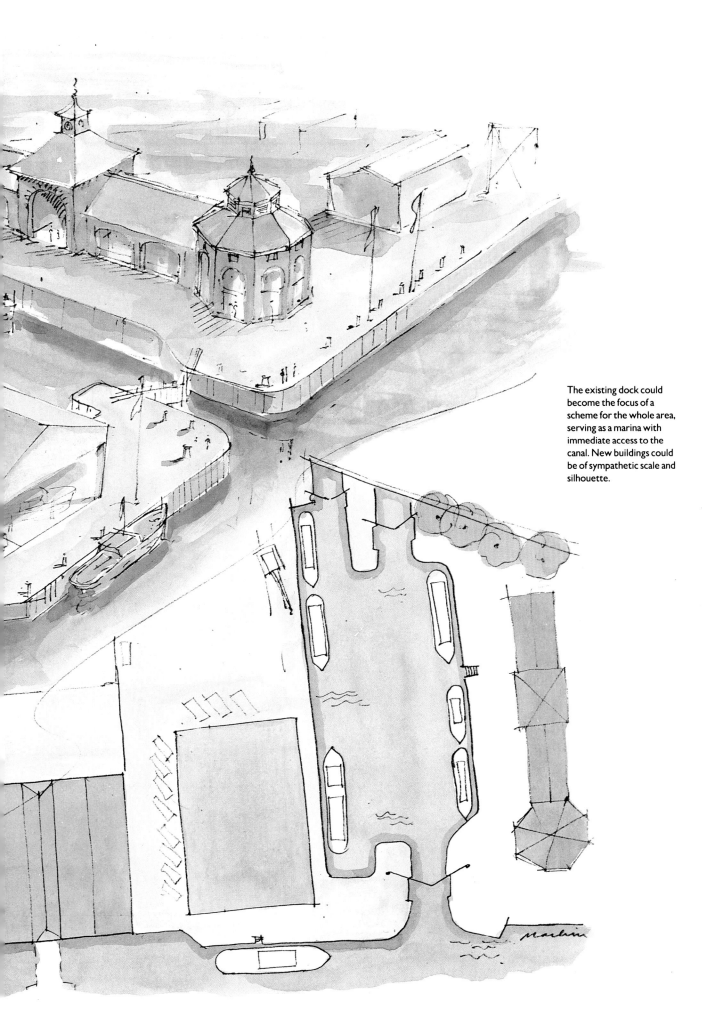

The existing dock could
become the focus of a
scheme for the whole area,
serving as a marina with
immediate access to the
canal. New buildings could
be of sympathetic scale and
silhouette.

Section

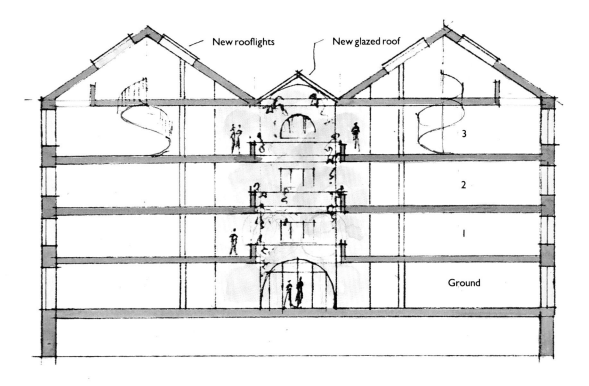

New rooflights    New glazed roof

3

2

1

Ground

Plan

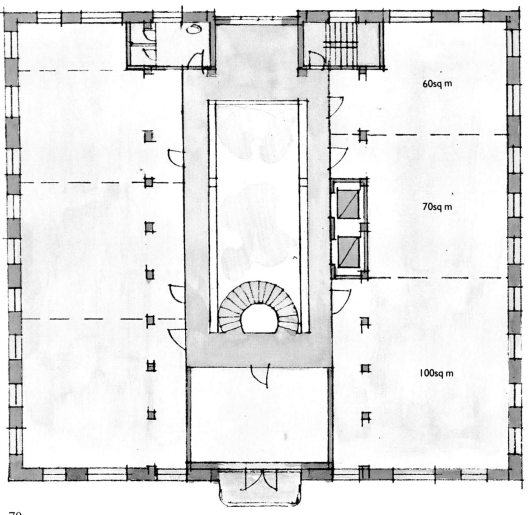

60sq m

70sq m

100sq m

Commercial success can depend upon a stylish, modern approach.

Historic structure integrated with contemporary detailing and lighting.

## Cressbrook Mill, Derbyshire

This supremely elegant classical mill is wonderfully situated in a very pretty valley in the Peak District National Park. There is an abundance of water with a mill pond behind the main building and a millstream running down the side.

Cressbrook was built in 1814-16, but textile production ceased about 1960 and since then its condition has deteriorated steadily. The mill is now empty and open to the elements; the surrounding area is used as a stonemason's yard. Though all the internal woodwork is in very poor condition, and will probably have to be stripped out, the masonry shell is substantially intact.

The aim of the scheme here is to take maximum advantage of the site. With its handsome pediment, Cressbrook has the look of an elegant classical mansion and here we show how it could become a superb country house hotel.

What is needed is a leap of the imagination which will wholly transform its surroundings without diminishing the rugged industrial grandeur of the building.

Though plainly detailed, it has a powerful presence and imposing formality. This could be developed, and indeed be made uniquely spectacular, by the creation of a formal garden on the axis of the south front in place of the existing derelict weaving sheds.

There is sufficient water not only to feed a long canal but the force is abundant enough to operate a powerful fountain. Simple terracing, lawns, and tree planting could create a very grand effect at relatively little cost.

Clearly there are not many places in the National Park where planning permission would be given for a substantial new hotel in a sylvan setting, so the proposition is all the more attractive.

Cressbrook is actually more easily adaptable than many country houses as a hotel as there is no problem in providing en-suite bathrooms. The floor plan is deep enough to provide generously proportioned bedrooms with bathrooms behind, opening off either side of a central corridor. Some 40-50 double bedrooms can readily be provided within the existing building.

On the north side there is ample space for car parking and an imposing entrance court. The split level plan means that the main reception rooms on the ground floor actually enjoy an elevated view over the formal gardens on the south side. Below, the dining room can have French windows opening directly onto the terraces. An indoor swimming pool can be provided in an existing building on the south west.

An alternative would be to restore Cressbrook for residential use. The Peak District is the most attractive residential area within easy distance of Sheffield and other South Yorkshire towns, yet for obvious reasons there is little chance of new houses being built in the National Park. With house prices rising sharply in the north, the economics of the operation become more attractive. The scheme shown here provides 13 houses in the lower part of the building with 10 flats above.

Cressbrook is listed Grade II* and is in a conservation area. Substantial grants are potentially available to support a suitable scheme.

The mill enjoys unparalleled views along one of the Peak District's most beautiful valleys.

Page 72: The approach along a simple country lane is as visually stimulating as a drive through 18th century parkland.

Water, the *raison d'etre* of the mill, becomes the key feature of the new formal layout. The mill stream is strong enough, not just to fill a large reflecting pool, but to propel a spectacular fountain.

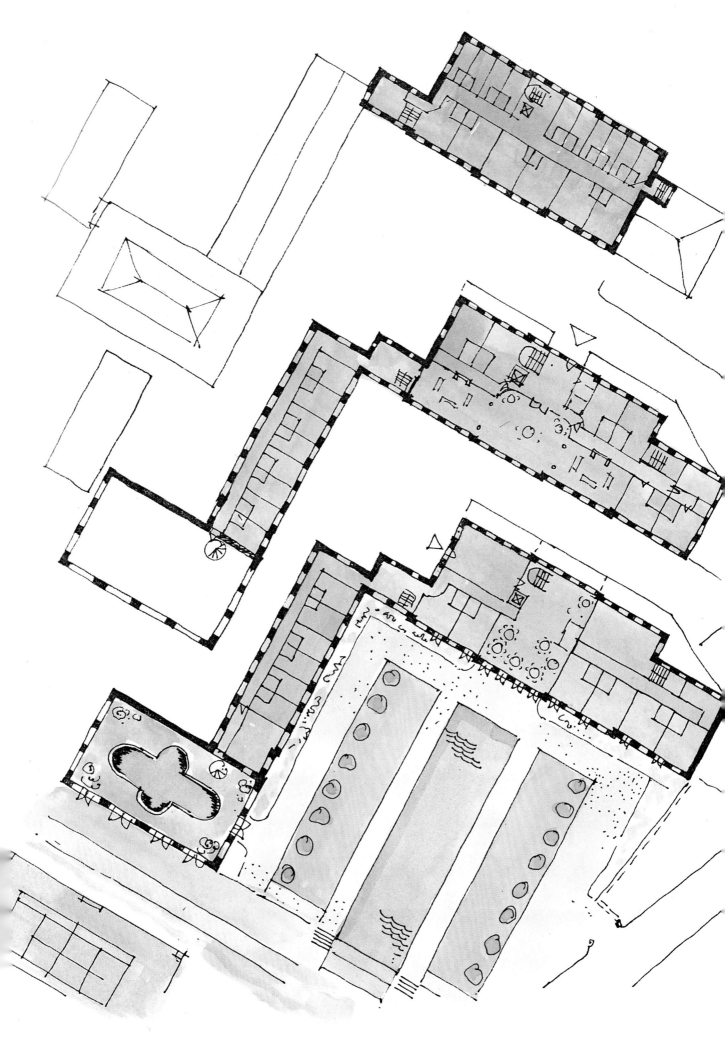

# Sufficient accommodation for a large, comfortable hotel

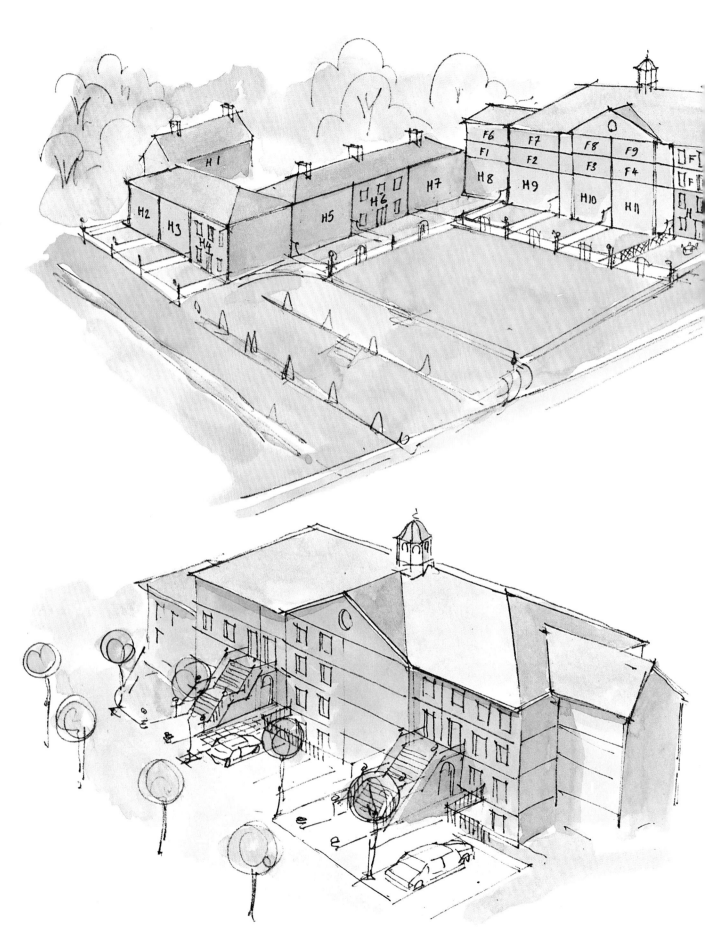

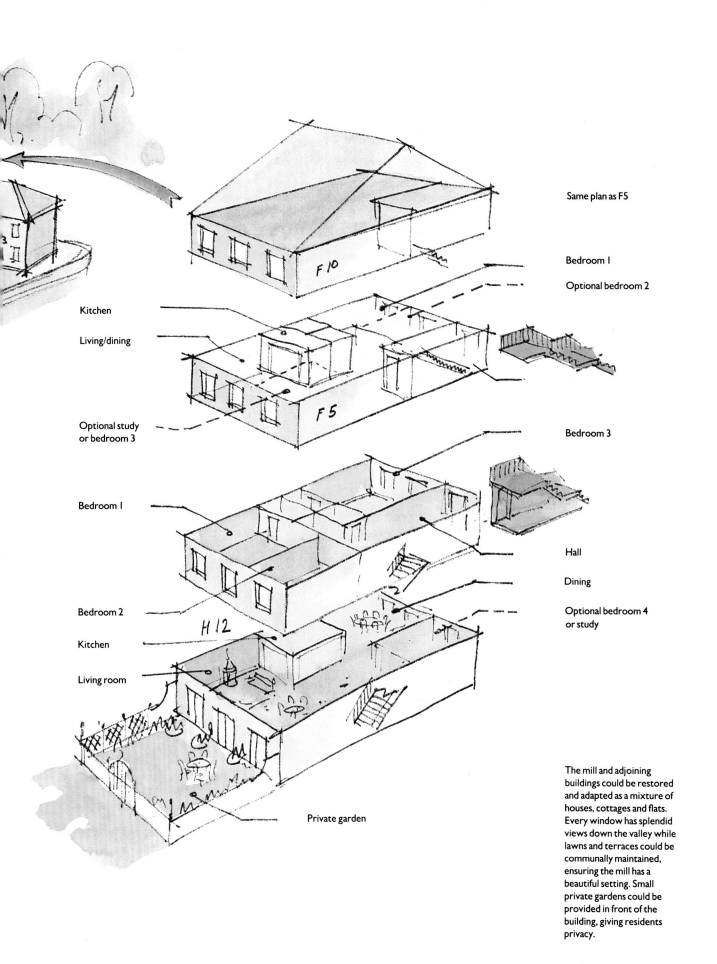

Same plan as F5

Bedroom 1

Optional bedroom 2

Kitchen

Living/dining

Optional study
or bedroom 3

Bedroom 3

Bedroom 1

Hall

Dining

Bedroom 2

Optional bedroom 4
or study

Kitchen

Living room

Private garden

The mill and adjoining buildings could be restored and adapted as a mixture of houses, cottages and flats. Every window has splendid views down the valley while lawns and terraces could be communally maintained, ensuring the mill has a beautiful setting. Small private gardens could be provided in front of the building, giving residents privacy.

79

The Tannery: view of the main block onto the street. This will be renovated and enlarged with a roof extension.

The internal courtyard is to be enlarged by the addition of a glazed roof. The end building will be replaced with a purpose built block.

80

## The Tannery, Bermondsey, London

This early Victorian industrial building has become redundant as a working tannery and is currently being refurbished and converted into an office and studio complex by Machin Architects.

The building itself is not significant enough in architectural terms to warrant preservation, however it represents an important example of an industrial building designed for the local fur processing industries historically linked to the Bermondsey area of London.

The retention of the building was justified commercially in site density terms, whereby the existing square footage of the building was much higher than a new build proposal would have been permitted to achieve. By creating an enlarged and glazed courtyard atrium and adding a replacement internal block, the layout of the floors has become cost effective and created a good net/gross ratio with an increased site density.

Finally, by keeping the architectural character of the building as a central focus of the design, with a naturally lit and spacious atrium, a positive marketing attraction for potential users has been created.

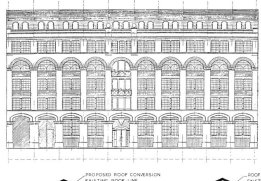

Elevation illustrating the additional storey.

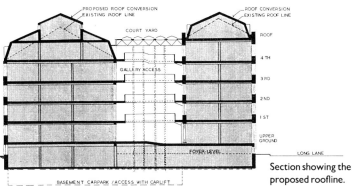

Section showing the proposed roofline.

Typical floor prior to conversion and fire protecting.

Below: typical floor plan with enlarged atrium. Blocks 1 and 3 are existing refurbished, blocks 2 and 4 are purpose built.

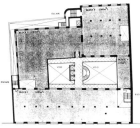

GRAND-PRIX
de l'A·C·F· 1908
Diep

# Smarter than New

A tiled panel on the Michelin building facade portrays images of the early days of competitive motoring.

# Conran sells style from a tyre depot

Left: Restored light fittings in the entrance hall.

Right: Detail of the restored stained glass window.

## The Michelin Building, London

The recent meticulous restoration of the Michelin building proves an important maxim: the best use for a historic building is usually, but certainly not always, its original use. The eye-catching front, built in 1909-11 to the design of Francois Espinasse, was a witty play on Michelin's imaginative advertising campaign. The recessed ground floor housed a tyre fitting bay, while behind was a touring office selling guides and maps. Over the years the building had been repeatedly extended and modernised, though happily the remarkable original tilework survived virtually intact. In 1972 permission was given to build a ten-storey office block behind the original building: fortunately Michelin decided to spend the money on a new factory instead. By 1985 Michelin decided the original building was no longer suitable for their offices – and indeed in an unneccesarily fashionable part of London for even the most illustrious of tyre depots.

So in August that year the building was sold to Sir Terence Conran and Paul Hamlyn who have made a point of restoring the original work to museum standards. The later additions on the back, simpler than the original but very much in keeping, have been substantially retained. Prestige uses have meant that the whole exterior has been cleaned and repaired to the highest standard, and necessary alterations and additions are beautifully designed and executed in the best materials.

The wrought-iron gates to the fitting bay have been reinstated to the original design; the tiled floor inside the bay has been preserved and repaired. The stained glass windows in the first floor Bibendum Restaurant, sent to Stoke for safekeeping in 1940, had been lost: these, too, have been expertly recreated following the original design. The domed glass cupolas, topping the corner turrets, have also been remade following Espinasse's drawings.

The main external change has been the insertion of a new glass shopfront to the Conran store, halfway along one flank. This rises the full height of the building and has the clean lines and materials associated with all Conran furniture. But it has been inserted with such care and precision that it actually adds to the interest of the building. The same can be said of the very good roof additions which give the whole block a new clean roofline, replacing some rather bitty earlier extensions. Once again the lines and proportions of the new work grow from the original with satisfying exactness. While Michelin had done good work in restoring their building in the 1970s, and generally maintained it with pride, they could never have justified the kind of investment, in terms of their own operation, that Terence Conran and Paul Hamlyn have been able to make. The restoration and conversion of the Michelin building as a prestige modern shop and office will, it is hoped, inspire other major entrepreneurs to look more closely at the potential of industrial buildings.

Page 84: The Michelin Building in London's Fulham Road. Conversion to shops and offices has prompted the most meticulous restoration.

### Ebley Mill, Stroud

No local authority in Britain has tackled the problem of its historic industrial buildings with such forthright determination as Stroud District Council. The Stroud Valley contains a chain of mills as large and grand as survive in almost any comparable rural Yorkshire valley. Ten years ago all were empty or beginning to deteriorate. The Council courageously determined to find uses for them all.

The flagship of the whole operation had been the conversion of Ebley Mill – one of the finest – as its own offices. The Council acquired the property in 1985 and four years later the last of the Council's departments, previously scattered across several buildings in Stroud and neighbouring Dursley, have been moved into the mill. Where 800 people toiled at crowded looms in the 1870s, 300 council employees now work in attractive, well-equipped modern offices.

There is a long history of milling on the site. A fulling mill called Maldon's is recorded as working at Ebley in 1469. The long range of the present building, known as the machine blocks, were begun in 1818; in 1862 GF Bodley, the great Victorian church architect, added a new wing at the end.

Listed Grade II*, the mill provides some 65,000 sq ft of floor space. The architects for the conversion are the Bristol-based practice Niall Phillips Associates.

The Council is highly computerised: every workspace has a computer terminal and one of the main challenges was to introduce the necessary cabling without destroying the character of the interiors. This was done through careful planning of the individual cable routes through the floor void.

The particular appeal of mill interiors lies in their open plan, with long vistas framed by columns running the whole length of each floor. Local authorities, however, tend to have a high requirement for cellular offices. This was reduced to a minimum by negotiation: and the use of glazed partitions further diminishes the impact of subdivision. Partitions are placed in such a way that rows of columns can still be seen uninterrupted.

When a new partition system is introduced in an old building, Niall Phillips points out, straight lines and sharp curves tend to highlight the fact that the existing walls, and perhaps even ceilings and floors, are out of plumb. An unhappy juxtaposition is created. He has minimised this in two ways: first by inserting a new level floor and, second, by using screens with glazed or rounded corners.

Many good mill interiors have been lost, cannibalized or simply concealed because they do not meet fire regulation requirements. Cast iron columns are frequently thought to perform badly in fires. Niall Phillips sent sections to the Building Research Establishment to be fire tested and was told they were resistant for the required period of one hour if coated with intumescent paint. The charring rate of the massive pitch pine beams proved to be sufficient without treatment. The main new requirement was the introduction of two new fireproof staircases. A sophisticated fire detection system has been introduced and the Council's insurers are reported to be completely happy.

The other main change is the introduction of a mezzanine floor in the roof of the Bodley block – for the architects' department – providing an extra 4,000 sq ft. Bodley's ties had to be cut, and a secondary tying structure introduced, but the original Queen posts have been preserved.

The attention to detail is admirable. The cast-iron window frames have been retained, slightly modified to provide opening lights. Outside, the Council has completed the composition by rebuilding the upper portion of the mill chimney.

At the time of completion, the Council is contesting a claim by the contractor, which has led to reports that the project has gone wildly over budget. Niall Phillips, however, is emphatic that the conversion will have cost no more than a new building and probably considerably less.

Ebley Mill before conversion.

Above: The main building at Ebley Mill with Stroud Council's major refurbishment underway.

Two views of the interior after conversion. The large open floors adapt excellently as flexible, modern office space.

### Britannia Hotel, Manchester

'The effect is of an enormous and luxurious bordello in a film by Fellini,' George Melly wrote of the conversion of the Britannia Hotel in Manchester from a High Victorian Warehouse. It says something of the hotel's rumbustious style that Melly should be thus quoted on a leaflet advertising weekend breaks. 'Inside,' he writes 'it's all purple and gold with a large staircase rising to a mirrored dome and sprouting circus-baroque columns en route.'

The 300 ft Watts Warehouse was designed by the Manchester architects Messrs Train and Magnall, with an elaborate stone facade, punctured by four towers suggesting a major public building or institutional headquarters. The Watts family's early fortune had been based on handspinning and weaving – their speciality was the handsome gingham. Their drapers' shop grew into a Drapery Bazaar, where individual weavers could rent a counter to display their wares. James Watts became High Sherriff of Lancashire, and Mayor of Manchester.

The family firm of S & J Watts continued until 1960, being absorbed shortly after in the Courtaulds group. The warehouse was sold for conversion as offices but the new owners went into liquidation. The Receiver applied for consent to demolish the building but a spirited campaign was initiated by Lady (Eleanor) Campbell-Orde to prevent this. In 1979 the warehouse was acquired by Britannia Hotels and permission for hotel use was granted.

The new 360-bedroom hotel, converted at a cost of £5 m, opened its doors on 1 March 1982. More than 300 permanent jobs have been created and the hotel has established itself not only among businessmen but won a place in Manchester's nightlife with restaurants, bars and two discothèques.

The converted warehouse contains a dramatic atrium, complete with bubble lift, such as is found in many new hotels.

### Niccol Centre, Cirencester

Here is a brilliant conversion of a disused brewery barrel store, providing a facility that is the first of its kind. A local surgeon had left a bequest for a capital project which would enrich the life of older people in Gloucestershire. A local councillor envisaged the building as an arts centre for people over 55, with studios, classrooms, workshops and a coffee bar, arranged around a central performance space. The conversion carried out by MacCormac Jamieson & Prichard at a cost of £200,000 has left stone walls and roof timbers exposed but given the whole space a stylistic unity characterised by the introduction of bold trellis balustrades. The 500 strong membership supports the running costs – some 23 courses are run each week, ranging from keep-fit to calligraphy, with all the facilities freely available to individual members for the rest of the time. Plays and other events are open to all and are held regularly in the theatre, which has great appeal thanks to its intimate proportions.

Stylish detailing in the new interior of the Niccol Centre.

An eye-catching and attractive new entrance has been created with the simplest of means.

At New Concordia Wharf spectacular modern apartments have been created in an old grain warehouse. All the industrial detailing has been retained to give character and the top of the chimney reinstated as a feature.

## New Concordia Wharf, London

Andrew Wadsworth was just 22 years old when he acquired the huge New Concordia Grain Warehouse on the south bank of the Thames. Though within a mile of Tower Bridge it stood in a very decayed area, of difficult access. He had the vision to see the potential of this remarkable position with wonderful views across the river and the neighbouring creek known as St Saviour's Dock.

The conversion is outstanding for the sympathetic treatment of the original fabric and the respect for authentic detail. The principal evidence that something spectacular has happened inside is the smart blue paintwork. Otherwise, original stone sets remain in the courtyard, exterior gangways and hoists have been retained; new windows have the knobbly detail of the cast-iron originals.

Car parking – an essential in this Dickensian area of narrow alleys, was provided in the basement. Ground floor offices are occupied by high-tech companies with rows of computer terminals visible through the windows, while above a range of large and small apartments have been created. The system adopted was to provide the new leaseholders with a front door and basic services – plumbing and electricity – but to leave all the internal fitting out – partitions, plastering, kitchens and bathrooms – to the buyers.

This was an ingenious way of resolving the problem of the very deep site. Each purchaser had to respond to the challenge in his own way – with the result that some highly original apartments have been created.

Normal building regulations require that new window area is equivalent to one-tenth of the floor space, at New Concordia the proportion is more like one-twentieth – but the sheer character of the old building has proved more than compensation for the restricted light.

In 1984 the cheapest studio flats sold for £24,000 (for 400 sq ft); large apartments ran to 1,800 sq ft and the very largest to 3,000 sq ft. In all, 60 flats and 24 workshops have been created. The big heavy internal timbers, which have a slow charring rate, have been retained; cast-iron columns have been fire-protected.

Following the outstanding success of the Concordia restoration most of the other surviving warehouses in the Shad Thames area have been purchased for conversion.

### New Mills, Wotton-under-Edge

Nothing frightens people about restoring an old building so much as the unknowns. What unexpected problem may be discovered after work has begun, increasing costs, and causing delays? Worst of all is when delays invoke penalty clauses on the contract.

At New Mills, the architects, Niall Phillips Associates, developed a system which they believe largely resolves this problem – and thus wins for the client the full financial benefit that using an existing building can provide.

The solution is simply to split the contract into two phases. The first will consist of basic repairs to the existing fabric – walls, floors and roof. This Niall Phillips calculates will usually be about one fifth, or one sixth, of the total cost. So, if the contract runs over by 20 per cent due to delays, any penalty is calculated on one fifth of the total cost, not the whole cost. Of course this means going out to tender twice, and possibly using two contractors, all of which may take slightly more time, and may increase the cost somewhat, but the benefit is to greatly reduce the risk.

The New Mills conversion is of special interest as an example of a very successful high-tech company deciding, partly for marketing reasons, that a restored mill could provide a prestigious headquarters and make a special impression on overseas clients.

Renishaw Metro specialise in producing robotic parts and systems for sophisticated machine tools – selling principally to Germany, Japan and the United States. The company purchased the property in 1980, initially for the production space offered by surrounding buildings. The first thoughts were towards developing new offices elsewhere on the site, but Niall Phillips Associates were able to show that the fine late 18th century mill, listed Grade II*, could provide first class accommodation – quite apart from the fact that listed building consent for demolition was unlikely to be granted.

Dating from the late 18th century, New Mills is one of the most romantically situated mills in the south of England. The brickwork has a fine patina, the central clocktower adds dignity and interest to a grandly symmetrical front, and the large mill pond immediately in front reflects the whole composition as memorably as any castle moat.

Inside, all the new work has a lightness and grace, contrasting beautifully with the sturdiness of the original structure. Tubular handrails, curved staircase and balcony landings, and semi-circular partitions create a new geometry that sits strikingly and happily with the existing fabric which is left exposed. New fire staircases are of lightweight construction, to avoid the possibility of different settlement.

Officially opened in July 1985, New Mills cost £1.2 m to convert, including some £250,000 spent on the structural works. The cost, excluding the work on the exterior, averaged £300 per square metre.

The uninterupted floor space allows for the flexibility required by a modern company.

Outside and inside, the
converted mill provides a
wealth of character and
good detail.

94

# A simple facelift has transformed this vast bland building into a spectacular landmark

## The Boston Design Center

Here is the world's most spectacular transformation of a vast, and literally white elephant. This huge military warehouse, eight storeys high and dating from 1919, has become the Boston Design Center, home of New England's burgeoning design and furnishings industry. Following conversion it provides 550,000 sq ft of showrooms for design and contract furnishing companies. The lower five floors are devoted to residential furnishing showrooms: the upper three floors display office furniture.

The whole venture demonstrates how, with imagination and flair, and not a great deal of money, a very utilitarian industrial structure can become as smart and chic as a very expensively fitted out new building – without compromising its essential character.

The Boston Design Center started life as a tank factory during World War II. Completed tanks were loaded straight onto ships in the harbour.

Modest expenditure on a new facade has transformed the Boston Design Center.

The Boston Design Center:
the new foyer.

The immense columns have
been sympathetically
incorporated into the new
scheme.

Page 97, above: The great
length of the building has
provided the opportunity
for dramatic vistas.

Page 97, below: On some
floors the long corridors are
broken up to create a feeling
of intimacy.

A new entrance has been made at the west end –
its design providing the logo for the whole
venture. Grand pilasters give style to the recessed
centre. A pediment containing the splendid
rhetorical gesture of a lunette, open to the sky,
crowns the elevation. Below, an imposing two-
storey entrance, at once massive and airy, rises to
another open pediment echoing the one above.
The subtle introduction of pale grey and pink
cladding adds tone and gives the front a
tailor-made look.

A 126 foot paved plaza has been laid out in front
of the building to ensure it proclaims the same
sense of luxury and richness the visitor will find
within. Inside, the 28 foot high lobby is
beautifully wainscotted in mahogany and anigre,
with verde antico and marble panels enclosing the
columns.

Each of the eight floors is organised along a
corridor stretching the length of the building
between the elevator cores in the east and west
wings. In the lower floors the corridors are
broken by stepping the showrooms forward so
the full length is not visible at any one point,
giving the internal streets a more intimate feel.
Above, long straight corridors reveal the full
extent of the larger office showrooms.

The Boston Design Center shows how a vast
sleeping giant of a building can become the
springboard for a wholly new venture. The
promotional literature boasts it is 'emerging as
the single place for the trade to do business for
both New England and Eastern Canada. Large
enough to house every important showroom,
those left outside the environment will suffer
from exclusion.'

The new centre stands just minutes from the
financial district and Logan Airport, in very much
the same position as Hunslet Mill does to the
centre of Leeds. What wonders Hunslet Mill
might not do for the Leeds rag trade.

The ultimate plus of projects like this, as with
Ernest Hall's Dean Clough Mills, can be
expressed in one word: *synergy*. A new showcase
has been created for a whole range of businesses
that vastly benefit from working and being
together.

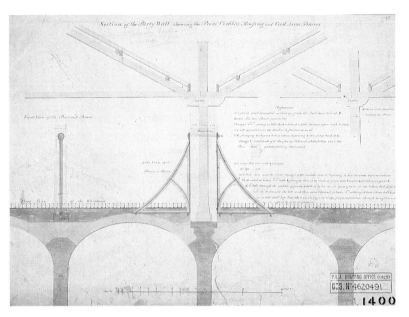

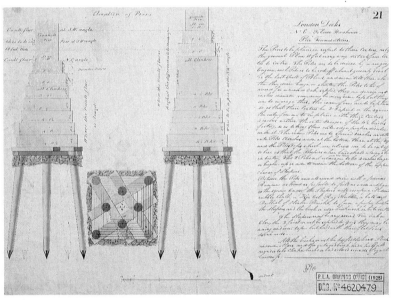

Above: Section through the skinfloor and vault showing the use of stone corbels and the manner in which the dividing wall is buttressed with cast iron braces.

Below: Elevation and plan showing method of constructing the brick and timber foundations below the granite vault columns.

## Tobacco Dock, London

The rescue of Tobacco Dock is due to the tenacity of two London entrepreneurs who quite simply fell in love with it. While Telford's great warehouses around St Katharine's Dock were destroyed one after another, while the great range of Regency warehouses in London Dock were flattened for News International, they kept the flame of interest alive in Tobacco Dock. It was a hard task. Few people had heard of it. Even fewer had seen it, for it was entirely concealed by high dock walls. Though increasingly derelict it was protected by a Grade I listing, and, with patience, Laurie Cohen and Brian Jackson put together a joint development company with Harry Neal, the builders, and brought in Terry Farrell, the apostle of the conservation plus approach – by which historic buildings are given a new lease of life with a strong but sympathetic injection of contemporary design.

Tobacco Dock, completed in 1814, was in effect a commercial fort – built to protect massive quantities of goods held in bond. Wines and spirits were stored in extensive stone and brick groin vaults below ground; the bales of tobacco were stacked above in single storey sheds. Very early on, however, tobacco gave way to huge quantities of sheepskins imported from Australia – hence the name Skinfloor by which the complex is sometimes known.

Terry Farrell's challenge was to subtly reverse the whole concept of the building – no longer to keep the public out, but to invite them in. The entrance, low-key but eye-catching, is a giant 'mousehole' – an elliptical arch in the boundary wall supported on the massive Egyptian columns Telford used in St Katharine's Dock.

You enter on the half level, being tempted both up and down simultaneously. The attraction on both floors are the long broad vistas right through the building with a glimpse of masts and rigging at the end.

What strikes at once is the generous size of everything – the broad, uncluttered concourses, the open, airy shops, bars and restaurants. By contrast to the closely packed grain of most London streets, markets and arcades, here the scale is American.

When complete, the new shopping centre will consist of six parallel ranges – two being open concourses, four containing retail units – and cross alleys. Though most of the complex is roofed, it is not enclosed and air conditioned. If it had been, fire regulations would have demanded that the complex be divided up into smaller areas – breaking up the vistas that are essential to the

# The character of the complex has been the magnet for the tenants

The entrance to Tobacco Dock has been designed so that upper and lower levels look equally inviting.

The new staircases are major focal points encouraging visitors to explore the different levels of shopping.

The drama of the vast
undercrofts formed a major
attraction to the developers.

The vaults showing the new
shops.

building's character. As it is there is free passage
along the concourses 24 hours a day.

On the upper level the remarkable roof structure
has been exposed to maximum advantage. The
cast-iron columns, which branch out like trees
were never used in the same way elsewhere; this is
in fact a timber type of construction adapted to
iron. Almost all the massive roof timbers have
been retained – being spliced where they had
rotted at the ends. Virtually all the shops on the
upper floor are open to the roof – increasing the
feeling of light and space.

Upper and lower levels are linked by new double
staircases – designed as freestanding features and
complemented by trellis pavillions in the adjacent
lightwells. Below, in the vaults, the atmosphere is
darker and more intimate – the boxes for the
security shutters are ingeniously designed to look
like lintels.

Phase I of the development, which opened in
March 1989, has cost £30 m. Phase II will take
the total to £50 m. Though the success of the
project cannot be gauged until all the units are let,
Tobacco Dock looks set to be a landmark in
showing how a major new shopping centre can be
imaginatively introduced in a historic building.

100

The sheer ingenuity and complexity of the structural elements helped ensure the survival of this building.

Looking along the new shopping mall at Tobacco Dock. Original constructional elements have been retained to give character.

101

## The Royal Agricultural Hall, London

The 'Aggie' provides another inspiring example of the way the vision, determination and tenacity of just one man can save a great industrial building. The Aggie's huge glass roofed halls rival the great train shed roofs of London termini like Paddington and St Pancras, but they had languished for 10 years, empty and steadily decaying. Repeated attempts had been made to obtain consent to demolish but Sam Morris, chairman of a local shop-fitting business, believed the Royal Agricultural halls had a future as an interior design centre – the English equivalent of great design emporia in San Francisco. Having convinced Islington Council and the GLC of the practicality of his proposals, he set up a development company and acquired the hall. One third of the funds for the project came from an Urban Development Grant – the remainder was raised commercially.

Built in 1861 to designs by Frederick Peak as a new base for the Smithfield Show, the hall was used for a whole range of events – industrial exhibitions, including the World Fair, sporting matches and grand balls.

Today it has once again taken on the role of multi-purpose venue – leased for events such as the Labour Party Conference.

Once again it shows that the large internal spaces of industrial buildings are highly adaptable and that their exposed ironwork, so far from being considered inelegant or outdated, forms a backdrop for a whole range of go-ahead organisations and vibrant events.

The exuberance of the architecture ensures the building is a well known landmark – a major attraction for the developer.

Page 103: The dramatic interior provides a memorable back drop to a whole range of events.

**Bliss Tweed Mill**

The beautiful north Oxfordshire countryside offers no greater surprise than Bliss Tweed Mill. Half sunk in a gentle fold of the landscape it has the most eccentric of all mill chimneys rising incongruously from a domed rotunda, which, to further discomfort the onlooker, is wilfully set off centre. This engaging gaucheness goes hand in hand with exuberance, notably in the paired arched windows of the top storey and the rich bracketed cornice above. Corner pavilions are crowned by balustrades and urns giving them, from a distance, the look of turrets.

The builder, William Bliss II, was evidently determined the architecture should live up to his name. Completed in 1873 the mill produced fine tweeds and fabrics for over 100 years. Production ceased in 1980 and it lay empty for eight years until plans for a residential conversion were approved. The mill itself has been restored as 34 apartments, with one, two or three bedrooms, while the adjoining Warping House has been converted into eight open plan duplex apartments. Original features such as the brick vaulted ceilings have been preserved. The original windows have also been retained, ensuring that externally the Grade II* listed mill is virtually unchanged.

The Wool House has been adapted as a leisure complex for the residents, with swimming pool, jacuzzi, squash court, billiard room and conservatory. The former Weaving House provides indoor parking for all the residents.

The venture, undertaken by Edward Mayhew, shows how all the buildings in a large mill complex can be restored and brought back to use on a commercial basis without damaging development in the land around. Purchasers are attracted to the mill because of its marvellous setting, unusual architecture and fine views.

This splendid scheme provides hope for numerous textile mills in rural areas, notably in the valleys around Stroud in Gloucestershire and towns such as Halifax and Huddersfield in the West Riding of Yorkshire. Such buildings may not be suited to modern industrial use, and industrial use would bring heavy traffic and possibly pollution, which would be unwelcome in a rural area. By contrast, residential use brings people who enjoy both the building and the surrounding countryside for its own sake.

All the ancillary buildings around the mill have been put to new uses.

Page 104: Bliss Tweed Mill. The new residents enjoy wonderful views over the surrounding countryside.

# Going, Going, Gone

4

In a few minutes the work
and memories of
generations can be reduced
to a pile of rubble.

Above: Anchor Mills, Paisley. Built in 1886 by Woodhouse and Morley of Bradford it has now been empty for five years. Its fine riverside site suggests potential for a residential conversion.

Right: Robinwood Mill, Todmorden, Lancashire. Built in the 1830s by the great engineer William Fairbairn it stands in an attractive valley, with spectacular moorland scenery all round.

Page 109: Sleaford Maltings, Lincolnshire. One of the grandest sets of maltings in the country, consisting of seven parallel ranges.

# The fate of these buildings hangs in the balance

Left: Globe Works, Sheffield. One of a number of fine classical factories in the city, it dates from the 1820s. Listed Grade II it long stood empty, but a scheme of conversion as workshops and activities associated with the cutlery industry is now complete.

Right: Sheaf Works, Sheffield. Dating from 1825 it is now disused, but plans have been drawn up for conversion as offices.

Below: Rodborough Buildings, Guildford, Surrey. The oldest multi-storey car factory in England. It is threatened by road development proposals.

Soho Mill, Thornton Road, Bradford. A problem for many years, its deteriorating condition has been a major concern to the local authority conservation team. It has recently changed hands and there is hope it may be converted into offices and workshops, although no firm plans have yet been put forward.

Below: Ashton Mill, Trowbridge. Dating from 1860 and listed Grade II.

This page:
The Camperdown Works in Dundee. One of the largest of the numerous mills which made Dundee the jute capital of the world. Built in 1861-68 by G A Cox, the complex covered 30 acres and employed 6,000 people. The 282 foot chimney, or stack, was added in 1865-66 by James McLaren. New uses are urgently needed to halt the further decay and demolition of Dundee's remarkable industrial heritage.

Page 113: The imposing red brick Edwardian cigarette factory at Bedminster, Bristol. Threatened by redevelopment plans.

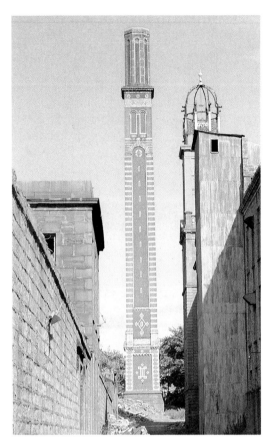

Brynmawr Rubber Factory, Gwent. Built in 1946-52 to the designs of the Architects Co-partnership, it is architecturally the most remarkable post-war building in Wales, deserving comparison with the Festival Hall on London's South Bank. Now disused, it offers large, uninterrupted areas of covered space, suitable for a range of shopping and leisure purposes.

Below: India Tyre Factory, Inchinnae, Paisley. Built in 1929-30 by Wallis Gilbert, architect of the Firestone Factory in London. Now empty and deteriorating.

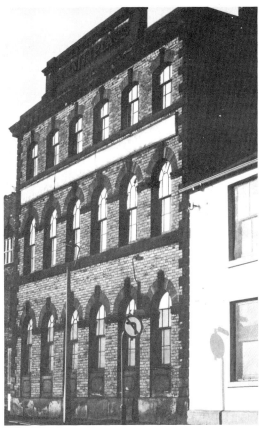

Left: The Cornish Place Works in Sheffield. Listed Grade II and now empty.

Tranmere Pumping Station on the outskirts of Birkenhead. This rugged engine house, dating from 1862, is now redundant and threatened with demolition.

Below: The Canal Wharf, Sheffield. Beautifully reflected in a canal basin, this palatially-proportioned warehouse has been steadily decaying for many years. A current scheme for restoring it as part of a shopping centre will engulf its setting.

Fall Lane Mill, Marsden, Yorkshire. A major local landmark, demolished following a fire.

Page 117: Loom breakers smashing machinery at James Nutter and Son's Bancroft weaving shed, Barnoldswick, Lancashire in 1979.

The final achievement of these demolished buildings may be to create a greater appreciation of those that survive

This page: Ellenroad Ring Mill, near Rochdale. One of the largest spinning mills in south-west Lancashire and the last big mill to be run on steam power. Following demolition of the mill in 1985, the Ellenroad Trust has preserved and restored the engine house and chimney.

Page 118: Queens Mill, Huddersfield. Demolished in 1977.

# Imagine what these buildings might have been today

Above left: Nahum's Mill, Salterhebble, near Halifax. Good Yorkshire mid-Victorian stone textile mill, now demolished.

Above right: The Cutler Street Warehouses, Whitechapel, London. Built for the East India Company, these were the largest group of Georgian warehouses in the world. The great zig-zag elevation along Middlesex Street, shown here, has been entirely demolished.

Sowerby Bridge Mill, near Halifax. A highly unusual brick mill, dated 1800, with mullion windows. Demolished because of its poor state of repair, it is a very sad loss.

Above: Bancroft Mill, Barnoldswick, Lancashire, during demolition in 1979.

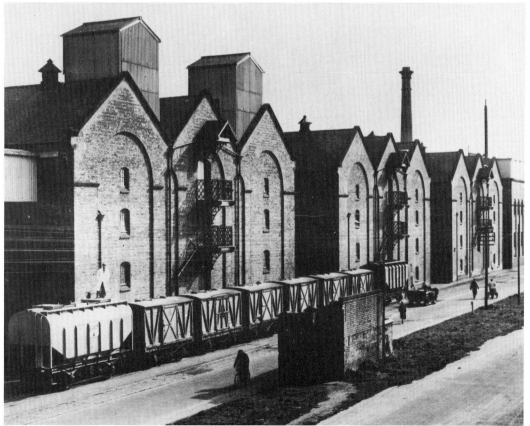

Shobnall Maltings, Burton-on-Trent, Staffordshire. The grandest range of Maltings in the country, it has been entirely demolished like most of Burton's unique brewing heritage.

121

This page: The Firestone Factory, Hounslow, West London. The finest front in the grand parade of Art Deco factories along the Great West Road. It was savagely mutilated over a bank holiday in August 1980 to forestall listing on the following Tuesday.

Page 123: The Brown and Pank Warehouse, Northampton. Built in 1877, it stood guard at the south entrance to the town. Demolished in 1976 for a lorry park for Carlsberg, whose historic brewery in Denmark is one of Copenhagen's leading tourist attractions.

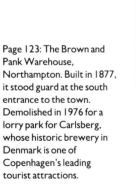

Belle Vue Mill in the
Weavers' Triangle, Burnley.
The chimney and engine
house, dating from 1868,
standing beside the Leeds
and Liverpool Canal shortly
before demolition in 1979.

**Index to Illustrations**

## Photographic Credits

Typeset by C Leggett & Son Ltd,
Mitcham, Surrey
Printed by WW Hawes Printers Ltd,
Elmswell, Suffolk